Independent and Unofficial

ULTIMATE

POKÉMON GO Handbook

STERLING CHILDREN'S BOOKS
New York

STERLING CHILDREN'S BOOKS
New York

An Imprint of Sterling Publishing
1166 Avenue of the Americas
New York, NY 10036

STERLING CHILDREN'S BOOKS and the distinctive
Sterling Children's Books logo are registered trademarks of
Sterling Publishing Co., Inc.

Distributed in Canada by Sterling Publishing
c/o Canadian Manda Group, 664 Annette Street
Toronto, Ontario, Canada M6S 2C8

For information about custom editions, special sales, and premium
and corporate purchases, please contact Sterling Special Sales at
800-805-5489 or specialsales@sterlingpublishing.com.
Manufactured in Canada
Lot #:
2 4 6 8 10 9 7 5 3 1
10/16

ISBN: 978-4549-2481-4

Authors: Clive Gifford, Anna Brett
Design: WildPixel Ltd.

So you want to be a Pokémon Trainer? Before you begin, you must agree to my safety code of conduct. Remember, a top Trainer is a safe Trainer!

- **Play the game in a group.** There's safety in numbers, and you can work as a team to find more Pokémon.

- **Plan your route and playing time.** This will mean you don't get lost, and an adult can come and find you if you're not home at the agreed time.

- **Pack your backpack.** Remember to take a drink and a snack with you. Trainers need to keep their strength up as well as Pokémon!

- **Stay alert at all times.** Don't run out into a road or walk near a cliff. Your Pokémon need you to be safe and well.

- **Play for fun.** There's no reason to go somewhere you wouldn't normally venture or to anger people who are not playing the game.

- **Charge up.** Playing the game uses up a lot of battery life, so take a spare charger with you. If your phone runs low, you can recharge it and call home.

CONTENTS

READY, SET, POKÉMON GO!

Welcome, Trainer. I am Professor Willow, and although my life is dedicated to studying Pokémon, I am also here to help train you. By completing the activities in this book, you will strengthen yourself and give yourself the chance to evolve into a better Pokémon Trainer.

As you begin to catch Pokémon, use this book to make notes about them. You can jot down where you caught them, what their CP level is, and how they did in battle. The facts will also help you identify their strengths and weaknesses. It's time to catch 'em all!

EYE SPY

CP stands for Combat Power

Pokédex # N/A	CP level: N/A

Professor Willow

- **Type:** Human
- **Profession:** Pokémon researcher
- **Favorite Pokémon:** Vaporeon
- **First Pokémon:** Rattata

GO FACT: Transfer your spare Pokémon to me in exchange for Candy!

Pokédex # 016	CP level: **27**

Pidgey

Write in the catch location and battle stats

- **Type:** Normal / Flying
- **Caught at:** *Local park*
- **Evolves into:** Pidgeotto
- **Battle stats:** *Defeated Caterpie in my first battle*
- **FA:** Tackle, Quick Attack
- **SA:** Aerial Ace, Twister, Air Cutter

GO FACT: Pidgey has a strong homing instinct and can always get back to its nest.

Before we begin, remind me of your name and then color in your outfit so I can add you to my list of students.

Please choose your style.

Write name below

Tristan Con

Write name below

....

YOUR FIRST CATCH

So you've downloaded the app, customized your character, and started exploring. Here's how to capture your first Pokémon.

The basic screen you'll come to is the Map View. This displays your character on a local map along with certain symbols and tools.

1

The compass shows you which way is north. Tap on the compass icon to switch between viewing northward and auto-rotation, which turns the map to follow the direction you are viewing.

2

Tall, colorful towers are Gyms—this is where things get serious! When you reach level 5, you'll be able to train and battle other Trainers' Pokémon here.

3

PokéStops are great places where you can get useful items such as Potions or Poké Balls. Sometimes, Pokémon are lurking nearby or you can pick up Pokémon Eggs—these can be hatched into new Pokémon for your collection (see page 20).

4

Your Trainer avatar represents you and shows your location on the screen.

5

Tapping the picture of your Trainer's head calls up your progress and any achievements made. You can alter how your Trainer looks at any time by tapping this option.

6

The Poké Ball–shaped circle is your button to go to the main menu. This allows you to access your Pokédex and any items you have, such as Incense, Potions, or Poké Balls.

7

The Sightings bar details any wild Pokémon lurking near your current position.

Your Trainer profile shows your level, your Gym team, and how many PokéCoins you have. The XP bar tells you how much experience you need to gain before you're due to level up.

Level 20

35000 / 50000 XP

50

START DATE:
08/08/2016

Team Valor

Charmander   Squirtle   Bulbasaur

YOUR FIRST POKÉMON

The game places a wild Pokémon close to you to get you started—either Squirtle, Charmander, or Bulbasaur. They will show up on the Map View screen so you can head toward them.

When you see a Pokémon on the Map View, tap it to start the capture screen. At the bottom of the screen is a Poké Ball. You have to drag this up the screen and release it with enough force to land on the Pokémon.

As you touch the ball, a target ring appears around the character. Green is an easy capture; yellow is slightly harder. High-level Pokémon have an orange or even a red ring, warning you that the Pokémon is very tough to catch. Your first capture should be easy, but others need a more accurate Poké Ball throw.

For the best chance of a capture, toss the ball when the target ring is at its smallest. A captured Pokémon appears in your collection and gains you Experience Points (XP).

Pikachu

PICK UP A PIKACHU

Did you know you can start your Pokémon GO adventure with Pikachu as your first Pokémon? Here's how. When you're first given a choice between Charmander, Squirtle, or Bulbasaur, walk away until your phone vibrates. You will see a prompt on your screen urging you to try to catch the Pokémon close by. Walk away another three to five times. The next Pokémon that appears close by should be Pikachu.

HUNTING POKÉMON

So you've captured one Pokémon. Chances are, you'll want many more. Here's how to go about it.

ON THE LOOKOUT

To start hunting for Pokémon, you'll need to take a walk. Different creatures are found in different areas (see pages 10–11) but, in general, there are lots of Pokémon in busy areas and public parks. Stay alert for changes on your Map View and try to play at different times of the day. A blank area of no interest can be a wonderland of Pokémon at a different time. Your mobile device should alert you and vibrate when wild Pokémon are close by.

WHAT'S IN THE BAG?

The Bag button (bottom right on the main menu screen) lets you access any possessions you have in the game. Some of these might help you capture Pokémon—different Poké Balls, Incense, or a Lure Module (see page 13), for example. Great Balls increase your chances of catching a Pokémon by half, while Ultra Balls double your chances. It's best to use these on harder-to-catch Pokémon— those surrounded by a red target ring during the capture sequence.

RAZZ BERRIES

Found from level 8 upward at PokéStops and as Level Up rewards, you can access a Razz Berry during a capture by tapping on the Bag icon. Select one, then toss it like a Poké Ball. Unlike Poké Balls, you can't miss with a Razz Berry. The Pokémon feeds on the Razz Berry and will be easier to capture with your next Poké Ball.

INCENSE

Every player starts with some Incense, and you can get more during the game—but use it wisely and sparingly. After deploying Incense, you have 30 minutes in which more Pokémon should appear near your location. Gamers report that if they walk around after using Incense, they encounter many more Pokémon than if they use it while standing or sitting in one place.

GRAB WHAT YOU CAN

When you start out, try to catch every Pokémon you can. If you get duplicates in your Pokédex, you can transfer them to Professor Willow in exchange for bonus Candy that will help you power up and evolve your creatures (see pages 18–19).

SWITCHING OFF

If you find it hard to catch Pokémon using Poké Balls, you can switch modes to make it easier. When a capture encounter occurs, it's usually in Augmented Reality (AR) mode, with the Pokémon projected in front of the real-world scene before you. Turning the AR switch off (usually found in the top-right corner of your screen) switches to a simpler mode with the Pokémon in the middle of the screen, making it easier to judge how far to toss a Poké Ball.

CATCH BONUSES

There are four different catch bonuses, from Nice to Curve.

Nice	When the ball lands at the moment the target ring is at its widest, you gain 10 XP.
Great	The ball lands in the middle of the target ring when it's half-size. This gives you a bonus of 50 XP.
Excellent	When the ball lands in the smallest target ring, you'll receive an extra 100 XP.
Curve	Throwing the ball in a bending path can gain you an extra 10 XP as well as give you a better chance of catching a Pokémon.

THROWING A CURVE BALL

To throw a Curve Ball, press and hold the ball with a finger on your right hand, then drag it in a small circle anticlockwise. You should see the ball start to spin and glimmer on the screen. Now toss the ball as you normally would, but aim a little to the side of your target (to allow for the spin) or arc it upward.

POKÉMON PLACES

There are more than 140 different Pokémon in Pokémon GO, arranged into 17 types. Each type tends to be found in different places, as this handy guide shows.

Don't worry if you can't get to a certain kind of location. Pokémon types can sometimes be found elsewhere or you may obtain a particular Pokémon by hatching an Egg.

Type	Pokémon				Places
Bug	Caterpie	Beedrill	Paras	Venomoth	Grassy areas, playgrounds, woods and gardens. Public parks are among the most common places to find these Pokémon.
Rock	Geodude	Onix	Kabuto	Aerodactyl	Parking lots, farmland, golf courses, nature trails, and quarries. Sometimes also found at large shopping centers.
Water	Squirtle	Krabby	Psyduck	Shellder	Almost always found near water, from outdoor swimming pools and ornamental ponds to lakes and oceans. Wetland areas such as marshes are also common spawning grounds.
Ice	Jynx	Cloyster	Lapras	Dewgong	Ponds, lakes, rivers, and other bodies of water, as well as glaciers, ski resorts, and sometimes large grassy areas.
Dragon	Dratini	Dragonair	Dragonite		These rare Pokémon can be hard to find but are mostly reported close to major places of interest, such as museums or landmarks. Some are also found around golf courses.
Fighting	Mankey	Machamp	Hitmonlee	Poliwrath	Almost always found in or near sports centers such as football fields, arenas, and stadiums. Sometimes found in numbers around larger Pokémon Gyms.
Grass	Bulbasaur	Oddish	Bellsprout	Paras	Found in gardens, small playing fields, farmland, city and town parks, hiking trails, and nature reserves.

Type	Pokémon				Where to find them
Psychic	Abra	Drowzee	Slowpoke	Mr. Mime	These mysterious Pokémon are mostly found in residential areas with a lot of houses, flats, or apartments. There are reports that they are also common around hospitals.
Electric	Pikachu	Voltorb	Electabuzz	Jolteon	Found most commonly in dry climates, around schools, and colleges, factories, and train stations. Some have been reported in residential areas and at libraries.
Fairy	Clefairy	Clefable	Jigglypuff	Wigglytuff	Local landmarks, such as famous buildings or statues, as well as beaches and coastlines.
Steel	Magnemite	Magneton			Generally found near train tracks and industrial buildings.
Fire	Charmander	Vulpix	Ponyta	Magmar	Built-up neighborhoods and farmland in dry areas.
Ground	Sandshrew	Diglett	Cubone	Rhyhorn	Open ground including farmland, parks, golf courses and woodlands.
Flying	Charizard	Zubat	Gyarados	Doduo	Grassy areas such as parks and large gardens. All Flying Pokémon are of two types, so use the Eye Spy pages to check out what other type a Flying Pokémon is to better track down its location.
Normal	Pidgey	Rattata	Jigglypuff	Spearow	Almost everywhere! They are the most common type of Pokémon, so expect to find them in your neighborhood, as well as when out and about in the country, shopping, or wandering around towns.
Ghost	Gastly	Haunter	Gengar		Spawning grounds for these rare Pokémon seem to be built-up areas after dark and in the early morning. They are also found in and around some churches and other places of worship.
Poison	Ekans	Nidoran (m/f)	Grimer	Koffing	Wetlands, marshes, and some lakes seem to have more of these Pokémon than other areas. They are also found in industrial areas.

POKÉSTOPS

Approach one of those blue cubes on your local map, and you'll find the spinning icon of a PokéStop. Here you can pick up handy spare objects, meet other gamers, and catch yet more Pokémon.

Walk toward a PokéStop until your Trainer avatar is surrounded by a circle. You are now within the stop's range.

Lucky Egg   Revive   Razz Berry

WHAT'S AT THE STOP?

Up to level 5, PokéStops will provide you only with extra Poké Balls and Eggs—not that they aren't welcome! After level 5, though, things get more interesting, with Lucky Eggs (see page 15), Razz Berries, Revives, and Potions all up for grabs.

SWIPE TO SPIN

Click the PokéStop and up pops a circular photo of its location in the real world. Swipe the circle sideways to make it spin. When it stops, bubbles containing handy items will pour out. Tap the bubbles to pop them one by one, or tap the X to add their contents to your Bag all at once.

POKÉSTOP REFRESH

After you've collected items from a PokéStop, its icon will change to purple, meaning you cannot collect any more goodies. It takes around five minutes for the stop to refresh back to blue. If another player visits a PokéStop before you, they will exhaust it only for themselves, not for you.

SAVE YOUR BATTERY

Hanging around PokéStops, swiping objects, and capturing Pokémon can quickly use up your battery. Here are some tips to increase your device's battery life:

- Turn down your screen brightness

- Close background apps not in use, especially busy social media apps like Facebook, Instagram, and Twitter

- Unless you're using Bluetooth, turn it off

- Go to Game Settings, found in the Pokémon GO main menu, and turn Music, Sound, or Vibration off

- In the Game Settings menu, click the Battery Saver option. Your device will let you know of any nearby PokéStops or Pokémon, but will dim the screen when it is down by your side in a horizontal position.

USING YOUR OWN LURES

You can buy Lure Modules from the Shop or receive them as Level Up rewards at levels 8, 20, 25, 30, 35, and 40. To use one of your own Lures, tap the PokéStop, and then tap the white bar underneath its name. If you have a Lure Module in your Bag, you can place it in the slot that is displayed.

DATA SAVER

If your mobile device doesn't come with unlimited data, try to visit PokéStops that are close to free Wi-Fi.

PETAL POWER

If a PokéStop is raining pink petals, it means that someone is using a Lure Module, which increases how frequently wild Pokémon appear there. Stay close to the PokéStop and there's every chance that a Pokémon will appear on your Map View. If two overlapping PokéStops have Lures operating at the same time, they act as a powerful Pokémon magnet for every Trainer nearby.

BOOST YOUR XP

Your Experience Points (XP) are crucial to success. If you don't build them up, you won't be able to move up the levels of the game and battle at Gyms or obtain and use new items. It will also be much harder to find and catch rarer Pokémon.

LEVEL UP TARGET
Each level requires you to gain a certain number of XP before automatically upping your Trainer level.

1220 XP

XP FOR FREE
Fortunately, there are a number of ways to boost your XP really easily right from the start of the game. If a PokéStop is near where you live, lucky you! Visit it regularly, because you will gain 50 XP every time you make a fresh visit and spin the circular photo. Shuttling between two or three PokéStops can really help XP mount up, especially when you're starting out. Training and battling at Gyms (see pages 26–31) can boost your XP as well.

LEVEL	XP NEEDED TO LEVEL UP
1	---
2	1,000
3	2,000
4	3,000
5	4,000
6	5,000
7	6,000
8	7,000
9	8,000
10	9,000
11	10,000
12	10,000
13	10,000
14	10,000
15	15,000
16	20,000
17	20,000
18	20,000
19	25,000
20	25,000
21	50,000
22	75,000
23	100,000
24	125,000
25	150,000
26	190,000
27	200,000
28	250,000
29	300,000
30	350,000

CATCH AND HATCH
Capturing a Pokémon will give you 100 XP, plus potential bonus points for your Poké Ball throw. Hatching a Pokémon from an Egg will gain you yet more XP (200 for a 2km Egg, 500 for a 5km Egg, and 1,000 for a 10km Egg), as will evolving a Pokémon (see page 19), which is worth a hefty amount: 500 XP.

If you catch or hatch a Pokémon new to your Pokédex, such as this Jigglypuff, you gain a further 500 XP.

LUCKY EGGS

If you grab a Lucky Egg, lucky you. These ace objects double the XP you earn from actions you make in the game for the next 30 minutes. So you need to be quick and smart. Lucky Eggs are occasionally found at PokéStops, and they can be bought with PokéCoins in the Shop, but you're also guaranteed one when you level up as a Trainer to levels 9, 10, 15, 20, and 25.

EGG SUCCESS

Good Pokémon GO gamers maximize the value of a Lucky Egg by planning a series of moves in advance. For example, if you have three PokéStops close to each other, shuttle between them to gain 100 XP (doubled from 50 by the Lucky Egg) for every visit plus up to 1,000 XP for catching Pokémon at the stops. And if you use a Lure Module or Incense to attract as many Pokémon as possible, your XP can really soar.

CP 171

Rattata

HP 28 / 28

| Normal | 4.56 kg | 0.32 m |
| Type | Weight | Height |

2110 STARDUST   123 RATTATA CANDY

POWER UP   1000   1

EVOLVE   25

Rattata needs 25 Candies to evolve into Raticate—see page 19.

CP 451

Raticate

HP 48 / 48

| Normal | 6.99 kg | 0.75 m |
| Type | Weight | Height |

2110 STARDUST   99 RATTATA CANDY

POWER UP   1000   1

EVOLVE YOUR XP

Another cool move is to build up a number of easy-to-evolve Pokémon in your Pokédex, such as Pidgeys, Caterpies, or Weedles. All three need just 12 Candies each to evolve, compared with the 100 required to evolve a Geodude into a Graveler. Make sure you have a number of these Pokémon in your Pokédex, as well as a lot of the right types of Candies, then evolve them while using your Lucky Egg.

LEVEL UP!

Once you start to level up, you'll unlock special items. Here's a handy chart that shows 'em all!

Level	Item	Effect
5	Potion	Heals an injured Pokémon by increasing its HP (Hit Points) by 20 points.
5	Revive	Revives a Pokémon that has fainted, restoring its HP to 50% of its maximum.
5	Incense	Lures wild Pokémon for 30 minutes—use it when you're planning to walk around.
8	Razz Berry	Feed one to a wild Pokémon to befriend it, making it easier to catch.
8	Lure Module	Attach this to a PokéStop to lure Pokémon for 30 minutes. You'll need to remain in the same place for maximum benefit.

Level	Item	Effect
9	Lucky Egg	Doubles the XP you earn over the next 30 minutes.
10	Super Potion	Heals an injured Pokémon by increasing its HP by 50 points.
12	Great Ball	Gives you a 50% higher chance of catching a Pokémon compared with using a regular Poké Ball.
15	Hyper Potion	Heals an injured Pokémon by increasing its HP by 200 points.
20	Ultra Ball	Doubles your chance of catching a Pokémon compared with using a regular Poké Ball.
25	Max Potion	Restores an injured Pokémon's HP to 100%.
30	Max Revive	Revives a Pokémon that has fainted, restoring its HP to 100%.
30	Master Ball	The most powerful ball—use it to catch super-rare and powerful Pokémon.

POWER UP AND EVOLVE

You don't stand still for long when playing Pokémon GO, and neither should your Pokémon! They have to progress and improve, and key ways of doing this are powering up by adding CP (Combat Power) or evolving them into new types of Pokémon.

COMBAT POWER

CP is an important measure of how good your Pokémon may be in battle. It's calculated behind the scenes by the app, but you can boost it by improving your own XP and making Level Ups as a Trainer. The curved line on a Pokémon's profile screen shows how high its CP can go in theory.

CP 608

Clefairy
HP 86 / 86

CP 184

Stardust +748

Spearow Candy +9

Spearow
HP 38 / 38

Normal / Flying	2.38 kg	0.35 m
Type	Weight	Height

POWERING UP

You can boost a Pokémon's CP by using Stardust. There is only one type of Stardust, and it works with every Pokémon. Every time you catch a Pokémon, you gain some Stardust—if the Pokémon is new to your Pokédex, the quantity tends to be higher. You also get a good amount of Stardust every time you hatch an Egg. A regular daily supply of Stardust can be delivered to you once you have moved up levels and are able to leave Pokémon to defend a Gym (see page 29).

EVOLVE

Almost all Pokémon can be evolved into a new, more powerful type, with higher CP and an array of different battle moves. For instance, a humble, cute Squirtle can be evolved first into a more powerful Wartortle and then later into a Blastoise equipped with two powerful water blasters that can hit small objects from more than 40 meters away.

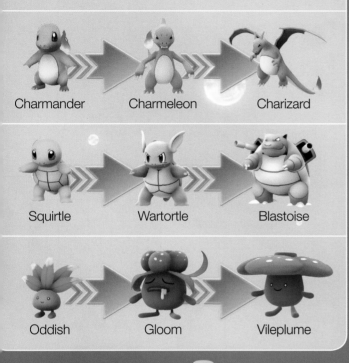

Charmander → Charmeleon → Charizard

Squirtle → Wartortle → Blastoise

Oddish → Gloom → Vileplume

HOW TO POWER UP OR EVOLVE

From Map View, tap the Poké Ball to enter the main menu, tap Pokémon, and then pick the Pokémon you wish to power up or evolve. Scrolling down reveals the Power Up and Evolve buttons, with how much Stardust and Candy it will cost you listed by the buttons. Tap the correct button to perform the task, and click Yes if you agree.

Most Pokémon cost 50 Candies of their own type to evolve. There are variations, however, as this chart shows.

12 Candies	25 Candies	100 Candies	400 Candies
Caterpie	Bulbasaur	Ivysaur	Magikarp
Weedle	Charmander	Charmeleon	
Pidgey	Squirtle	Wartortle	
	Rattata	Nidorina	
	Nidoran ♀	Nidorino	
	Nidoran ♂	Gloom	
	Oddish	Poliwhirl	
	Poliwag	Kadabra	
	Abra	Machoke	
	Machop	Weepinbell	
	Bellsprout	Graveler	
	Geodude	Haunter	
	Gastly	Dragonair	
	Eevee		
	Dratini		

EGGS AND HATCHING

Getting an Egg is pretty easy —just head to PokéStops until you pick one up. You can hold a maximum of nine Eggs at once.

0/5 km
Use an incubator to incubate this Egg.

START INCUBATION

0/5 km
Walk to hatch this Egg.

HOW TO HATCH

You'll need an Incubator to hatch your Egg in. Luckily, you're equipped with one right from the start of the game and it lasts forever. Swipe right from your Pokémon screen to view the Eggs you have. Select the one you want to hatch, and tap the Start Incubating menu option.

Pinsir

EGG INCUBATORS

If you want to hatch more Eggs, though, you'll need to buy more Incubators. Each can hatch three Eggs before it's no longer usable. Remember that you get one free Incubator as a Level Up reward at each of these levels: 6, 10, 15, and 25. Getting to level 20 gives you two free Incubators while level 30 rewards you with three for free. Awesome!

GO THE DISTANCE

In order to incubate and hatch an Egg, you have to travel a certain distance. Most Eggs require 5km but some, such as Jigglypuff and Squirtle, only need 2km. Others, such as Jynx and Electabuzz, need 10km.

WALK THE WALK

These 2km, 5km, and 10km distances are real-world measures of how far you have to walk to make your Egg hatch into a Pokémon, so put your shoes on and start moving around. On the Egg screen, look below each Incubator to see how far you've walked for each Egg.

Do not play Pokémon GO while driving.

OK

CARS NOT ALLOWED

Pokémon GO has a speed detector built into the game code, so don't think you can catch a ride or hop onto your bike and race along with your digital device to speed up the hatching process. Gamers report a 20–32km/h speed limit, so a brisk walk or gentle trot should be fine. Some sneaky gamers have strapped their smartphones to robotic vacuum cleaners to get them to cover the distance—but where's the fun in that?

2km Eggs	10km Eggs
Bulbasaur	Aerodactyl
Caterpie	Chansey
Charmander	Dratini
Clefairy	Eevee
Geodude	Electabuzz
Jigglypuff	Hitmonchan
Magikarp	Hitmonlee
Pidgey	Jynx
Pikachu	Kabuto
Rattata	Lapras
Spearow	Magmar
Squirtle	Omanyte
Weedle	Onix
Zubat	Pinsir
	Scyther
	Snorlax

RECORD BREAKERS

Pokémon GO has smashed records since it was launched on July 6, 2016, and it has encouraged gamers to become record breakers themselves. Read on for some of the record highlights in the Pokémon GO story so far.

MOST POPULAR DOWNLOAD

Since its release, Pokémon GO has destroyed app records. It's the fastest-selling app ever at Apple's store, and it has been downloaded more than 100 million times from the Google Play store for Android devices. With 23 million daily users in the US, it's the country's most popular mobile game.

GET 'EM ALL

In July 2016, 28-year-old Nick Johnson filled his Pokédex with all 142 Pokémon currently available in the United States. He claimed to have walked 153.2km to secure all the characters, his first being Squirtle and his last being Omastar, which he evolved himself.

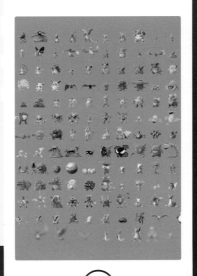

ROUND-THE-WORLD QUEST

Although Niantic, Inc. has not stated it officially, it's thought that four rare Pokémon can each only be found on one continent of the world. Johnson had secured Tauros in North America before a travel company sponsored him to fly to Paris, France, to collect Mr. Mime. He headed to Hong Kong to secure Farfetch'd and finally to the Australian city of Sydney to secure Kangaskhan.

MADRID MEET-UP

More than 5,000 Pokémon GO fans met up in the Puerta del Sol square in Madrid in July 2016 with the aim of becoming record breakers. It was the biggest crowd ever gathered together in one place for a Pokémon hunt. They beat more than 2,000 gamers who had turned out for the Pokémon GO Walk in Sydney, Australia, earlier in the same month.

5,000: MADRID, SPAIN

2,000: SYDNEY, AUSTRALIA

 = 500 people

FIRST COUNTRIES TO GET POKÉMON GO

Gamers in New Zealand, Australia, and the United States were the first to be able to download the game on July 6, 2016. The game has since been released in dozens of other countries. The first country to ban the game was Iran—spoilsports!

Australia

United States

New Zealand

GYMS AND TEAMS

Reaching level 5 means that I'll introduce you to Pokémon Gyms. Now's your chance to join one of three teams: Valor, Instinct, or Mystic.

CHOOSE A TEAM

Choose carefully, because, as of now, you cannot change teams later. You may decide to pick the same team as your friends so that you can work together to take over a Gym.

TEAM VALOR

Color: Red
Leader: Candela
Mascot: Moltres

Candela believes that Pokémon are stronger than humans and wants to increase their power even further.

TEAM MYSTIC

Color: Blue
Leader: Blanche
Mascot: Articuno

Blanche believes that Pokémon possess great wisdom and that calm analysis of a situation always wins out.

TEAM INSTINCT

Color: Yellow
Leader: Spark
Mascot: Zapdos

Spark believes in the power of Pokémon's intuition and instinct, which stems from how they hatch.

AT THE GYM

Look out for the tall, colorful towers near and far—they're usually located in places of interest or busy parts of your neighborhood. As you get closer, you should see a Pokémon sitting on top of the Gym structure.

GYM DETAILS

Tapping on a Gym will show you its name, which team is in charge, and its Gym level. It will also show you how many Pokémon it contains and their types, as well as which Trainers are inside.

ENTER A FRIENDLY GYM

If you see a Gym of the same colour and team as your own, you may be able to enter it. If you can't, it may be because the Gym needs to level up. A level 2 Gym, for example, can only accept two Pokémon, while a level 4 Gym can accept four. You can level up a Gym by increasing its Prestige. Turn the page to see how.

CLAIM AN OPEN GYM

The easiest way to gain a Gym is to claim an empty or open one. Most Gyms are colored yellow, red, or blue (one of the three teams' colors), but some are gray. These are empty Gyms. To claim one, tap the Gym on your map and, at the bottom of the screen, touch the Add Pokémon button.

Then pick one of your Pokémon to be added to the Gym. Choose carefully, because the Pokémon you select won't return to your Pokédex until it is knocked out of the Gym. In a level 1 Gym, you can place only one Pokémon.

GYM PRESTIGE AND TRAINING

So you're at the Gym. Before you get down to battle, you need to learn more about what makes a Gym tick, its status, and how to practice your own Pokémon sparring skills.

WHAT'S PRESTIGE?
When you tap on a Gym, check out the number in the upper-left-hand corner. This is a Gym's Prestige, and it determines the level of a particular Gym.

Gym level	1	2	3	4	5	6	7	8	9	10
Minimum Prestige required	0	2,000	4,000	8,000	12,000	16,000	20,000	30,000	40,000	50,00

PRESTIGE AND POWER
A Gym's power and importance are determined by its Prestige level. The higher the level, the more Pokémon the Gym can hold and the harder it will be for an opposing team to conquer and take control. Prestige can be raised when you or a player on the same team adds a Pokémon to the Gym. It's also increased every time a Trainer at the Gym wins a battle. Prestige can also be lost, though, by losing battles to players from a team other than your own.

Severndroog Castle
Gym level 3

6000 / 8000

CHARIZARD
CP 1860

IN TRAINING

To train at a Gym, get in range of a friendly Gym and tap it to enter. Another Trainer's Pokémon will appear in front of you. Make a note of its type and its CP rating—you want to start off battling Pokémon with a much lower CP than your own. Learning about which Pokémon types are stronger and weaker against a rival type (see pages 32–33) will help you make a good match before you start the battle in the arena screen.

Winston Churchill Memorial Garden
Gym level 2

2000 / 4000

DROWZEE
CP 150

Click the boxing glove icon at the bottom right, and you'll be able to choose a Pokémon from your Pokédex to train at the Gym.

Electabuzz   Blastoise
734   76   589

XP BOOST

The XP you gain from a training battle equals $1/10$ of the Prestige earned by the Gym during the contest. So if the Gym gains 500 Prestige points, you enjoy a 50 XP bonus. The maximum Prestige boost from defeating a single opponent in training is 1,000, equal to a 100 XP bonus. Raising the Prestige of a Gym that you intend to add a Pokémon to will make it harder for rival teams to take over.

Top Tip
Put your second-strongest Pokémon in a Gym. This lets you train against it with your strongest and win, raising the Gym's Prestige.

EARLY ESCAPE

If you want to end a battle early, you can run away from the Gym by tapping the runner button located at bottom right. If your Pokémon loses while fighting a friendly Pokémon in training, it will not faint, but it will return to your collection with its health down to just 1 HP and will need a Potion to heal it.

GYM FULL?

Each time a Gym wins a battle, it gains Prestige, even if the battle is between two players of the same team. So some players choose to battle friendly Pokémon regularly to build enough extra Prestige to move the Gym up a level. This means it will have a spare slot to accept another Pokémon—a clever way of joining a friendly Gym that was previously full! Remember that only a Pokémon that has 100% of its HP can be added to a Gym.

Squirtle   97   Charmander
CP 13   36

Not very effective...

Messages let you know how successful an attack was, so you can build up experience and know which moves to pull against a particular opponent.

BATTLING A RIVAL GYM

Now that you've trained and learned how to pick and use Pokémon to win bouts at a friendly Gym, you'll want to go all out and take on a rival Gym. Good luck!

PICKING A FIGHT

If you see explosions and signs of battle on the platform and tower on your Map View, it means another Trainer is already fighting at that Gym. But there's no need to wait politely. You can join in and fight alongside them.

CROWNING GLORY

To see all of the Pokémon guarding a Gym, swipe left. Pokémon stationed at Gyms are shown in order of their CP, from weakest to strongest. You will fight the weakest Pokémon first and the strongest last. The strongest is known as the Gym Leader and is marked with a crown icon on the Gym home screen. You must select six of your Pokémon to battle the Gym's creatures, and you can alter the order yours will appear in battle.

KNOCKED OUT, SWAPPED IN

HP (short for Hit Points) is the measure of your Pokémon's resistance to attacks. When it reaches zero, your Pokémon will faint and is called back to your collection. The next one of your six replaces it and joins the battle. If all six of your Pokémon faint, you lose, but if you have a battling Pokémon whose attacks are not working well, you can quickly swap it out for another of your six by tapping the two-arrow button toward the bottom right of the screen.

LOSS OF PRESTIGE

Gyms lose Prestige for every Pokémon a challenger defeats. Defeating all the Trainers at one Gym will lower its Prestige by 2,000. In many cases, this will demote the Gym down a level, meaning it can hold one Pokémon fewer. You'll also gain a major XP boost to your Trainer status.

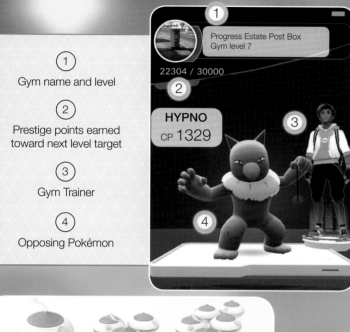

1. Gym name and level

2. Prestige points earned toward next level target

3. Gym Trainer

4. Opposing Pokémon

Incense	8 Incense	25 Incense
🌐 80	🌐 500	🌐 1250

BIG BONUSES

Gyms and battling can seem complicated, and it may take time to wrestle control of opposing Gyms, but the rewards are worth it. Aside from boosts to your XP and Trainer level, there are also valuable bonuses for holding a Gym successfully. Every 21 hours, visit the Shop and tap on the Shield button to receive 10 PokéCoins and 500 Stardust for every Pokémon you have stationed at a Gym.

If you manage to keep plenty of Pokémon securely in Gyms, these rewards can mount up quickly and help you buy handy items such as Incense (above), Lucky Eggs, Lure Modules, and upgrades to storage items and Pokémon.

YOU WIN!

Winston Churchill Memorial Garden
Gym level 1

0 / 2000

☆

Pokémon Defeated:	1
XP	+150
Gym Prestige	-2000

MULTIPLE ATTACKS

You may not completely defeat a Gym in one battle. Lowering the Prestige level of a Gym will often require multiple attacks. If you are successful again and again, the Gym will plummet until it is a level 1 with a Prestige of zero. This means the Gym is totally defeated. Well done!

Once defeated, the Gym tower will lose the color of its former team because it is no longer under their control. Now's the time to add one of your Pokémon to claim the Gym for you and your team, be it Mystic, Instinct, or Valor.

BATTLING

Pokémon GO battles occur in real time, meaning you need rapid reactions and must make quick decisions to do well.

ATTACK!

Tap your opponent's Pokémon again and again to fire off your Pokémon's basic move, known as its Fast Attack. A second type of move gets charged up as you battle and perform a lot of Fast Attacks. This is your Pokémon's Special Attack. It can be fired only when there's enough charge. To unleash a Special Attack, long-press your Pokémon. These attacks can be devastating when used at the right time.

①
Countdown timer

②
Status bar indicates health of a Pokémon

③
When one blue bar is full you can unleash a Special Attack

④
Incoming attack

DODGE 'EM

You can dodge a Pokémon's attacks with a quick, well-timed swipe of the screen either left or right. Look for the yellow flash around your opponent, which means an attack is coming, and time your swipe. If you are too early or too late, your Pokémon will take a hit. Be sure to work on your dodges in training, because it can take a lot of plays before you're confident in avoiding an attack.

PICK YOUR MOMENT

Special Attacks aren't always the right move during a battle. Even a super-powerful Special Attack such as Cross Chop, Body Slam, or Power Whip can leave your Pokémon open to attack because it takes time for your Pokémon to recover, during which it cannot dodge. Many gamers will use certain Special Attacks only to finish off an opponent.

Top Tip

Be alert right at the start of a battle to dodge an immediate attack from your opponent.

EYE ON THE CLOCK

Battles last up to 120 seconds, with the countdown timer reset every time a Pokémon that is defending a Gym faints. Other things to keep an eye on include the status bar of your own Pokémon and that of your opponent's. The bar goes from green to yellow to red as a Pokémon's HP falls. Once in the red, the Pokémon is critical and may faint and lose at any moment.

PLAN AHEAD

Battles may be fast and furious, but you can plan calmly beforehand as you build your knowledge. For example, scout out the opponents at a Gym in advance to learn which types have an advantage over others. Keep an eye out for mismatches such as one of your Pokémon being vulnerable to most of the Gym's Pokémon types. And check your Pokémon's profile screens to see what attacks they have at their disposal. One might have a Fast Attack, such as Metal Claw, Psycho Cut, or Fire Fang, that you particularly like.

KNOW YOUR ENEMY

CP is important when picking Pokémon to train or battle a rival Gym, but type can often be crucial, especially in early battling. For example, an underpowered Squirtle may defeat a Geodude with a higher CP, because Water-type Pokémon are strong against Rock types. Use this handy chart to pit your Pokémon against opponents who are less likely to exploit their weaknesses.

Normal Type
Strong Against: No advantages
Weak Against: Fighting, Rock, Steel, Ghost

Bug Type
Strong Against: Grass, Psychic
Weak Against: Fire, Flying, Rock, Ghost, Steel, Fairy

Poison Type
Strong Against: Grass, Fairy
Weak Against: Ground, Psychic, Steel, Rock

Grass Type
Strong Against: Water, Ground, Rock
Weak Against: Fire, Ice, Poison, Flying, Bug, Dragon

Water Type
Strong Against: Fire, Ground, Rock
Weak Against: Electric, Grass, Dragon

Fire Type
Strong Against: Steel, Bug, Ice, Grass
Weak Against: Rock, Water, Ground, Dragon

Steel Type
Strong Against: Ice, Rock, Fairy
Weak Against: Fire, Water, Fighting, Ground

Ground Type
Strong Against: Fire, Electric, Poison, Rock, Steel
Weak Against: Water, Grass, Ice, Bug

Fighting Type
Strong Against: Normal, Ice, Rock, Steel
Weak Against: Flying, Psychic, Fairy, Poison

Rock Type
Strong Against: Fire, Ice, Flying, Bug
Weak Against: Water, Fighting, Ground, Steel

Fairy Type
Strong Against: Fighting, Dragon
Weak Against: Poison, Steel, Fire

Electric Type
Strong Against: Water, Flying
Weak Against: Ground, Steel, Grass, Dragon

Psychic Type
Strong Against: Fighting, Poison
Weak Against: Psychic, Bug, Ghost

Ghost Type
Strong Against: Psychic, Ghost
Weak Against: No disadvantages

Dragon Type
Strong Against: Fire, Water, Electric, Grass
Weak Against: Ice, Dragon, Fairy, Steel

Ice Type
Strong Against: Grass, Ground, Flying, Dragon
Weak Against: Fire, Water, Fighting, Rock, Steel

Flying Type
Strong Against: Grass, Fighting, Bug
Weak Against: Electric, Ice, Steel, Rock

MAKING MOVES

Knowing what moves are available to your collection of Pokémon can really help you select the right creature to triumph in battles and Gym takeovers. Here are some of the most damaging moves plus several top tips.

WATCH YOUR WEAPONS

Check your Pokémon's profiles, especially if you have several of the same Pokémon. Different Pokémon of the same type can have different attacks available in battle. So, you might have two Gengar with different CP, but the one with lower CP may have a Shadow Claw, which is a stronger Fast Attack than the other Gengar's Sucker Punch.

TOP 10 FAST ATTACKS

Attack	Type	DPS (Damage per second)	Available to
1. Pound	Normal	12.96	Clefairy, Clefable, Jigglypuff, Wigglytuff, Drowzee, Chansey, Jynx, Ditto
2. Metal Claw	Steel	12.7	Sandslash, Kingler
3. Psycho Cut	Psychic	12.28	Kadabra, Alakazam
4. Scratch	Normal	12	Charmander, Charmeleon, Charizard, Sandshrew, Paras, Diglett, Meowth, Persian, Mankey, Kabuto
5. Water Gun	Water	12	Wartortle, Blastoise, Psyduck, Golduck, Slowpoke, Slowbro, Seel, Horsea, Seadra, Staryu, Starmie, Vaporeon, Omanyte, Omastar
6. Wing Attack	Flying	12	Charizard, Pidgeotto, Pidgeot, Golbat
7. Bite	Dark	12	Wartortle, Blastoise, Raticate, Abrok, Nidoran ♀, Nidorina, Nidoqueen, Zubat, Golbat, Meowth, Growlithe, Arcanine, Gyarados, Aerodactyl

8. Dragon Breath	Dragon	12	Seadra, Gyarados, Dratini, Dragonair, Dragonite
9. Fire Fang	Fire	11.9	Arcanine
10. Shadow Claw	Ghost	11.58	Haunter, Gengar

TOP 10 SPECIAL ATTACKS

1. Cross Chop	Fighting	30	Psyduck, Mankey, Primeape, Machop, Machoke, Machamp
2. Stone Edge	Rock	25.81	Nidoqueen, Dugtrio, Machamp, Graveler, Golem, Onix, Hitmonlee, Rhydon, Kabutops
3. Blizzard	Ice	25.64	Tentacruel, Dewgong, Cloyster, Seadra, Lapras
4. Body Slam	Normal	25.64	Ratatta, Nidoran ♀, Nidoran ♂, Clefairy, Vulpix, Jigglypuff, Meowth, Growlithe, Eevee, Snorlax
5. Power Whip	Grass	25	Bulbasaur, Ivysaur, Bellsprout, Weepinbell, Lickitung, Tangela
6. Hurricane	Flying	25	Pidgeot
7. Megahorn	Bug	25	Nidoking, Rhydon, Seaking
8. Solar Beam	Bug	24.49	Ivysaur, Venusaur, Vileplume, Parasect, Victreebel, Exeggutor, Tangela
9. Fire Blast	Bug	24.39	Charizard, Ninetales, Arcanine, Ponyta, Rapidash, Magmar, Flareon
10. Hyper Beam	Bug	24	Raticate, Wigglytuff, Electrode, Lickitung, Aerodactyl, Snorlax, Dragonite

STABs

When you use an attack of the same type as your Pokémon, you get a Same Type Attack Bonus (STAB). Examples include an Electric-type Pokémon such as Pikachu or Voltorb using a Thunderbolt, which is an Electric-type attack, or a Caterpie or other Bug-type Pokémon unleashing a Bug Bite. All STABs increase the power of the attack by 25%.

DOUBLE TROUBLE

Some Pokémon are classified as two types and will obtain a STAB by using a move of either type. For example, a Lapras receives a STAB if it uses a Water-type or an Ice-type attack.

HEALING AND MEDALS

Your poor Pokémon may take a pummeling at a Gym and need to have their injuries healed or be revived if they have fainted. Luckily the game allows you to give them a helping hand!

Potion   Super Potion   Hyper Potion   Max Potion

POTION POWER
Potions restore HP to injured Pokémon. Basic Potions, which you can get at PokéStops starting at level 5, restore 20 HP. That's fine for some Pokémon, but not all. You may have to use multiple Potions or deploy a Super Potion, which restores 50 HP, a Hyper Potion that adds 200 HP or a Max Potion, which restores all of a Pokémon's HP.

CANDY TO THE RESCUE
If one of your Pokémon needs help and you're out of Revives, you can use Candy instead. Spend the Candy to power up or evolve the stricken Pokémon, and it will come back to life with all of its HP restored.

Revive   Max Revive

REVIVES
If your Pokémon loses all its HP, it will faint and be in need of a Revive. Like Potions, these items are found at PokéStops and as rewards for Level Ups (see pages 16–17). They come in two types: The most common, Revive, restores 50% of a Pokémon's HP, while Max Revive restores all of it. Unfortunately, you won't encounter Max Revives until you reach level 30.

There's even a medal for catching one of the game's most famous characters, Pikachu. Catch three Pikachu to get a bronze medal and catch 50 to get silver.

MARVELOUS MEDALS
Different achievements reward you with Trainer medals. You can view any medals you've won in your Trainer profile. Some of the most common are to the right.

General Achievement Medals

Name	Achievement	Bronze	Silver	Gold
Jogger	Walk a distance	10km	100km	1,000km
Kanto	Register a Pokémon in your Pokédex	20	50	100
Collector	Capture Pokémon	30	500	2,000
Scientist	Evolve Pokémon	3	20	200
Breeder	Hatch Eggs	10	100	1,000
Backpacker	Visit PokéStops	100	1,000	2,000
Battle Girl	Win Gym battles	10	100	1,000
Ace Trainer	Train at a Gym you control	10	100	1,000

Pokémon-Type Medals

Name	Achievement	Bronze	Silver	Gold
SchoolKid	Capture Normal-type Pokémon	10	50	200
Black Belt	Capture Fighting-type Pokémon	10	50	200
Bird Keeper	Capture Flying-type Pokémon	10	50	200
Punk Girl	Capture Poison-type Pokémon	10	50	200
Ruin Maniac	Capture Ground-type Pokémon	10	50	200
Hiker	Capture Rock-type Pokémon	10	50	200
Bug Catcher	Capture Bug-type Pokémon	10	50	200
Hex Maniac	Capture Ghost-type Pokémon	10	50	200
Depot Agent	Capture Steel-type Pokémon	10	50	200
Kindler	Capture Fire-type Pokémon	10	50	200
Swimmer	Capture Water-type Pokémon	10	50	200
Gardener	Capture Grass-type Pokémon	10	50	200
Rocker	Capture Electric-type Pokémon	10	50	200
Psychic	Capture Psychic-type Pokémon	10	50	200
Skier Tale Girl	Capture Ice-type Pokémon	10	50	200
Dragon Tamer	Capture Dragon-type Pokémon	10	50	200
Fairy Tale Girl	Capture Fairy-type Pokémon	10	50	200

GO SECRETS

Buried deep within the app are some lesser-known tips and features that can add more fun, allow you to personalize the game, or enhance your gameplay.

NAME CHANGE
Following a game update, it's now possible to change your Trainer name, but you can do it only once. Tap on the Poké Ball on the main screen, select Settings, and tap on Change Nickname.

NICKNAME GAME
You can slightly personalize a Pokémon's name so that it displays differently on its screen by using HTML codes, just like you would when building a Web page. Add the html text codes on each side of the nickname. To make the name bold, for example, enter <b> and </b> on each side.

EVOLVING EEVEE
If you have an Eevee Pokémon and enough Eevee Candies (25) to evolve it, you know there are three types it can turn into: Jolteon, Flareon, or Vaporeon. But did you know you can pick which one it becomes by nicknaming your Eevee before evolving it? Type in the nickname "Sparky" if you want it to evolve into a Jolteon, "Rainer" if you require a Vaporeon, or "Pyro" if you need a Flareon. Make sure the first letter is a capital letter, otherwise the trick won't work.

Eevee

Jolteon   Vaporeon   Flareon

FIND OUT MORE

Part of the fun of Pokémon GO is learning about all the creatures, types and attacks available to you as you progress through the game. Some online sources are useful in speeding up your knowledge of what goes on in the game. Pokémon GO databases list all of the Fast and Special Attacks, as well as other stats and data for individual Pokémon.

Lucky Egg

Lure Module

Poké Balls

Bag upgrade

Incense

Egg Incubator

INDIVIDUAL VALUES

Hidden below each Pokémon's CP and HP are a set of figures describing how each Pokémon performs, develops, and levels up over time. These secret stats, called Individual Values (IV), determine a Pokémon's attack, defense, and stamina—its ability to keep going and recharge its power. This means that two Pokémon with the same CP could actually defend or attack differently, so some dedicated Pokémon GO gamers have developed IV calculators that you can use on the Internet. Here are two of them:

https://pokeassistant.com/main/ivcalculator

www.azurilland.com/tools/iv-calculator

IVs may not make much difference at the start, but they might make a big difference to how powerful your Pokémon is by the time it's powered up and fully evolved.

GO SHOPPING

PokéCoins can be bought with real-world money at a rate of 100 coins for $0.99, as well as earned by keeping Pokémon at Gyms. They can be spent at the Shop in different ways. For example, you can store up to 250 Pokémon at one time, but buy the Storage Upgrade at the Shop for 200 PokéCoins to hold more.

Item for Sale	Cost
20 Poké Balls	100 PokéCoins
100 Poké Balls	460 PokéCoins
200 Poké Balls	800 PokéCoins
1 Incense	80 PokéCoins
8 Incense	500 PokéCoins
25 Incense	1,250 PokéCoins
1 Lucky Egg	80 PokéCoins
8 Lucky Eggs	500 PokéCoins
25 Lucky Eggs	1,250 PokéCoins
1 Lure Module	100 PokéCoins
8 Lure Modules	680 PokéCoins
Egg Incubator	150 PokéCoins
Bag Upgrade	200 PokéCoins
Storage Upgrade	200 PokéCoins

SO YOU THINK YOU KNOW POKÉMON GO?

So you think you're a Pokémon GO expert now? See how much you really know by taking this multiple-choice quiz. The answers are on page 80.

1. How many times can you use an Egg Incubator bought at the Shop?
a) Once ○
b) Three times ●
c) Nine times ○

2. What type of Pokémon are Squirtle and Poliwag?
a) Rock ○
b) Fire ○
c) Water ●

3. At which level can you join a Gym?
a) Level 5 ●
b) Level 10 ○
c) Level 15 ○

4. By how many points does a Hyper Potion increase a Pokémon's HP?
a) 200 ●
b) 50 ○
c) 1,000 ○

5. Which color represents Team Valor?
a) Yellow ○
b) Blue ○
c) Red ●

6. What object can you feed to a wild Pokémon to befriend it and make it easier to capture?
a) Razz Berry ●
b) Super Potion ○
c) Lure Module ○

7. For how long does a Lucky Egg double your XP?
c) 10 minutes ○
b) 30 minutes ●
c) 60 minutes ○

8. What is the name of the special item that revives a Pokémon that has fainted, restoring its HP to 100%?
a) Great Ball ○
b) Hyper Potion ○
c) Max Revive ●

9. Which Pokémon is listed as number one in the Pokédex?
a) Jigglypuff ○
b) Bulbasaur ●
c) Caterpie ○

10. How many Poké Balls can you buy for 100 PokéCoins?
a) 20 ●
b) 50 ○
c) 100 ○

11. Which Rock-type Pokémon evolves into Graveler?
a) Geodude ●
b) Onix ○
c) Pinsir ○

12. Blanche is the leader of which team in Pokémon GO?
a) Team Valor ○
b) Team Instinct ○
c) Team Mystic ●

13. How many Candies does it take to evolve a Pidgey to a Pidgeotto?
a) 4 ○
b) 12 ●
c) 36 ○

14. How many Prestige points must a level 9 Gym have at minimum?
a) 12,000 ○
b) 25,000 ○
c) 40,000 ●

15. Which team has the Legendary Bird Zapdos as its mascot and is led by Spark?
a) Team Valor ○
b) Team Instinct ●
c) Team Mystic ○

16. Which of the following can Oddish evolve into?
a) Gloom ●
b) Vileplume ○
c) Venomoth ○

17. Poison-type Pokémon are not strong against which one of the following Pokémon types?
a) Grass ○
b) Fairy ○
c) Psychic ●

18. How much Stardust do you receive at the Shop for each Pokémon you have at a Gym?
a) 100 ○
b) 500 ●
c) 1,000 ○

19. How many Candies does it take to evolve an Eevee?
a) 25 ○
b) 50 ●
c) 100 ○

20. What medal type is awarded for evolving multiple Pokémon?
a) Scientist ●
b) Kanto ○
c) Breeder ○

EYE SPY LOGBOOK

You should have started collecting Pokémon by now, Trainer. How many do you have in your backpack? Start filling in the details here.

Can you catch 'em all and complete the Eye Spy panels in this book?

CP = Combat Power

FA = Fast Attacks

SA = Special Attacks

Pokédex # 001   CP level:

Bulbasaur

- **Type:** Grass / Poison
- **Caught at:**
- **Evolves into:** Ivysaur
- **Battle stats:**

- **FA:** Tackle, Vine Whip
- **SA:** Power Whip, Sludge Bomb, Seed Bomb

GO FACT: The plant bulb on its back provides it with energy.

Pokédex # 004   CP level:

Charmander

- **Type:** Fire
- **Caught at:**
- **Evolves into:** Charmeleon
- **Battle stats:**

- **FA:** Scratch, Ember
- **SA:** Flamethrower, Flame Burst, Flame Charge

GO FACT: The flame at the end of its tail indicates its mood and health.

Pokédex # 005   CP level:

Charmeleon

- **Type:** Fire
- **Caught at:**
- **Evolves into:** Charizard
- **Battle stats:**

- **FA:** Scratch, Ember
- **SA:** Flamethrower, Flame Burst, Fire Punch

GO FACT: Charmeleon is vicious and seeks out opponents.

Pokédex # 002   CP level:

Ivysaur

- **Type:** Grass / Poison
- **Caught at:**
- **Evolves into:** Venusaur
- **Battle stats:**

- **FA:** Vine Whip, Razor Leaf
- **SA:** Power Whip, Solar Beam, Sludge Bomb

GO FACT: Exposure to sunlight adds to its strength and helps the bulb grow.

Pokédex # 003   CP level:

Venusaur

- **Type:** Grass / Poison
- **Caught at:**
- **Evolves into:** N/A
- **Battle stats:**

- **FA:** Vine Whip, Razor Leaf
- **SA:** Solar Beam, Sludge Bomb, Petal Blizzard

GO FACT: Its flower emits a soothing scent that attracts Pokémon.

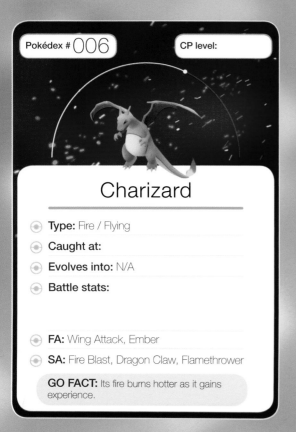

Pokédex # 006   CP level:

Charizard

- **Type:** Fire / Flying
- **Caught at:**
- **Evolves into:** N/A
- **Battle stats:**

- **FA:** Wing Attack, Ember
- **SA:** Fire Blast, Dragon Claw, Flamethrower

GO FACT: Its fire burns hotter as it gains experience.

Pokédex # 007   CP level:

Squirtle

- **Type:** Water
- **Caught at:**
- **Evolves into:** Wartortle
- **Battle stats:**

- **FA:** Tackle, Bubble
- **SA:** Aqua Tail, Aqua Jet, Aqua Pulse

GO FACT: It can withdraw into its shell to sleep.

Pokédex # 008

CP level:

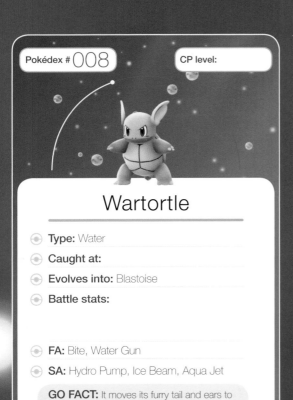

Wartortle

- **Type:** Water
- **Caught at:**
- **Evolves into:** Blastoise
- **Battle stats:**

- **FA:** Bite, Water Gun
- **SA:** Hydro Pump, Ice Beam, Aqua Jet

GO FACT: It moves its furry tail and ears to help it balance when swimming.

Pokédex # 009

CP level:

Blastoise

- **Type:** Water
- **Caught at:**
- **Evolves into:** N/A
- **Battle stats:**

- **FA:** Bite, Water Gun
- **SA:** Hydro Pump, Ice Beam, Flash Cannon

GO FACT: Blasts of water from its cannons can pierce steel and concrete.

Pokédex # 012

CP level:

Butterfree

- **Type:** Bug / Flying
- **Caught at:**
- **Evolves into:** N/A
- **Battle stats:**

- **FA:** Bug Bite, Confusion
- **SA:** Psychic, Bug Buzz, Signal Beam

GO FACT: Its wings are covered in poisonous powder.

Pokédex # 013

CP level:

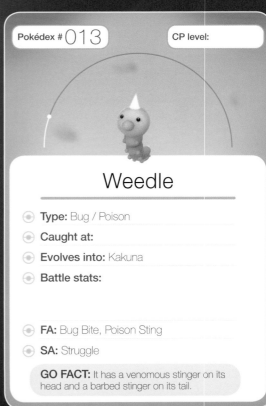

Weedle

- **Type:** Bug / Poison
- **Caught at:**
- **Evolves into:** Kakuna
- **Battle stats:**

- **FA:** Bug Bite, Poison Sting
- **SA:** Struggle

GO FACT: It has a venomous stinger on its head and a barbed stinger on its tail.

Pokédex # 010 — CP level:

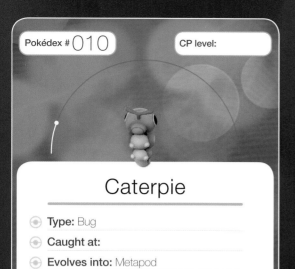

Caterpie

- **Type:** Bug
- **Caught at:**
- **Evolves into:** Metapod
- **Battle stats:**

- **FA:** Bug Bite, Tackle
- **SA:** Struggle

GO FACT: Its bright-red antennae release a powerful stench.

Pokédex # 011 — CP level:

Metapod

- **Type:** Bug
- **Caught at:**
- **Evolves into:** Butterfree
- **Battle stats:**

- **FA:** Bug Bite, Tackle
- **SA:** Struggle

GO FACT: A hard outer shell protects the soft body inside.

Pokédex # 014 — CP level:

Kakuna

- **Type:** Bug / Poison
- **Caught at:**
- **Evolves into:** Beedrill
- **Battle stats:**

- **FA:** Bug Bite, Poison Sting
- **SA:** Struggle

GO FACT: It has two barbed arms in the middle of its body.

Pokédex # 015 — CP level:

Beedrill

- **Type:** Bug / Poison
- **Caught at:**
- **Evolves into:** N/A
- **Battle stats:**

- **FA:** Poison Jab, Bug Bite
- **SA:** Sludge Bomb, X Scissor, Aerial Ace

GO FACT: Poison is stored in the stingers on its limbs.

Pokédex # 016

CP level:

Pidgey

- **Type:** Normal / Flying
- **Caught at:**
- **Evolves into:** Pidgeotto
- **Battle stats:**

- **FA:** Tackle, Quick Attack
- **SA:** Aerial Ace, Twister, Air Cutter

GO FACT: Pidgey has a strong homing instinct and can always get back to its nest.

Pokédex # 017

CP level:

Pidgeotto

- **Type:** Normal / Flying
- **Caught at:**
- **Evolves into:** Pidgeot
- **Battle stats:**

- **FA:** Wing Attack, Quick Attack
- **SA:** Aerial Ace, Twister, Air Cutter

GO FACT: It has amazing vision, enabling it to spot prey, like Exeggcute.

Pokédex # 020

CP level:

Raticate

- **Type:** Normal
- **Caught at:**
- **Evolves into:** N/A
- **Battle stats:**

- **FA:** Bite, Quick Attack
- **SA:** Hyper Beam, Hyper Fang, Dig

GO FACT: Its teeth are strong enough to gnaw through steel.

Pokédex # 021

CP level:

Spearow

- **Type:** Normal / Flying
- **Caught at:**
- **Evolves into:** Fearow
- **Battle stats:**

- **FA:** Peck, Quick Attack
- **SA:** Drill Peck, Aerial Ace, Twister

GO FACT: Its loud shrieks warn others of danger.

Pidgeot

Pokédex # 018   CP level:

- **Type:** Normal / Flying
- **Caught at:**
- **Evolves into:** N/A
- **Battle stats:**

- **FA:** Wing Attack, Steel Wing
- **SA:** Hurricane, Aerial Ace, Air Cutter

GO FACT: It can fly faster than the speed of sound.

Rattata

Pokédex # 019   CP level:

- **Type:** Normal
- **Caught at:**
- **Evolves into:** Raticate
- **Battle stats:**

- **FA:** Tackle, Quick Attack
- **SA:** Body Slam, Hyper Fang, Dig

GO FACT: Its sharp fangs allow it to eat anything.

Fearow

Pokédex # 022   CP level:

- **Type:** Normal / Flying
- **Caught at:**
- **Evolves into:** N/A
- **Battle stats:**

- **FA:** Steel Wing, Peck
- **SA:** Drill Run, Aerial Ace, Twister

GO FACT: It can fly for an entire day without landing.

Ekans

Pokédex # 023   CP level:

- **Type:** Poison
- **Caught at:**
- **Evolves into:** Arbok
- **Battle stats:**

- **FA:** Poison Sting, Acid
- **SA:** Gunk Shot, Sludge Bomb, Wrap

GO FACT: Ekans preys on Pidgey and Spearow eggs.

Arbok

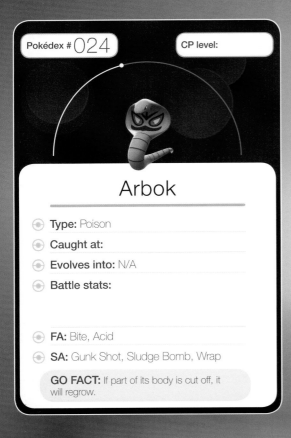

Pokédex # 024

CP level:

- ⊚ **Type:** Poison
- ⊚ **Caught at:**
- ⊚ **Evolves into:** N/A
- ⊚ **Battle stats:**

- ⊚ **FA:** Bite, Acid
- ⊚ **SA:** Gunk Shot, Sludge Bomb, Wrap

GO FACT: If part of its body is cut off, it will regrow.

Pikachu

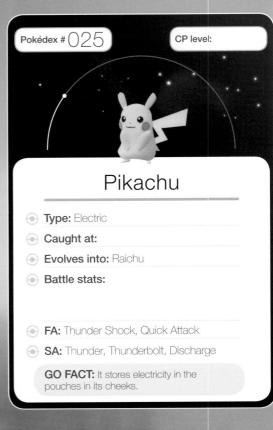

Pokédex # 025

CP level:

- ⊚ **Type:** Electric
- ⊚ **Caught at:**
- ⊚ **Evolves into:** Raichu
- ⊚ **Battle stats:**

- ⊚ **FA:** Thunder Shock, Quick Attack
- ⊚ **SA:** Thunder, Thunderbolt, Discharge

GO FACT: It stores electricity in the pouches in its cheeks.

Sandslash

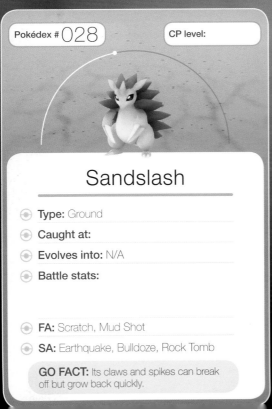

Pokédex # 028

CP level:

- ⊚ **Type:** Ground
- ⊚ **Caught at:**
- ⊚ **Evolves into:** N/A
- ⊚ **Battle stats:**

- ⊚ **FA:** Scratch, Mud Shot
- ⊚ **SA:** Earthquake, Bulldoze, Rock Tomb

GO FACT: Its claws and spikes can break off but grow back quickly.

Nidoran ♀

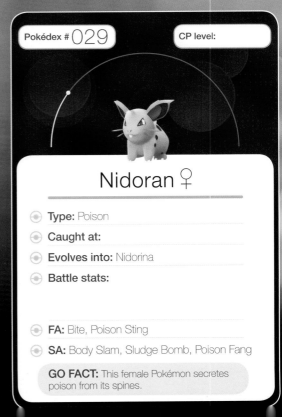

Pokédex # 029

CP level:

- ⊚ **Type:** Poison
- ⊚ **Caught at:**
- ⊚ **Evolves into:** Nidorina
- ⊚ **Battle stats:**

- ⊚ **FA:** Bite, Poison Sting
- ⊚ **SA:** Body Slam, Sludge Bomb, Poison Fang

GO FACT: This female Pokémon secretes poison from its spines.

Pokédex # 026 CP level:

Raichu

- **Type:** Electric
- **Caught at:**
- **Evolves into:** N/A
- **Battle stats:**

- **FA:** Spark, Thunder Shock
- **SA:** Thunder, Brick Break, Thunder Punch

  GO FACT: It glows in the dark thanks to all the electricity it stores.

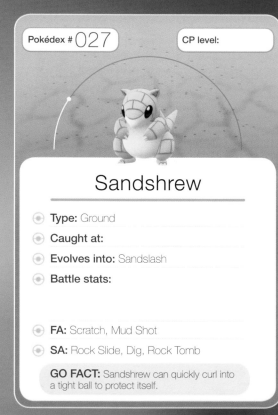

Pokédex # 027 CP level:

Sandshrew

- **Type:** Ground
- **Caught at:**
- **Evolves into:** Sandslash
- **Battle stats:**

- **FA:** Scratch, Mud Shot
- **SA:** Rock Slide, Dig, Rock Tomb

  GO FACT: Sandshrew can quickly curl into a tight ball to protect itself.

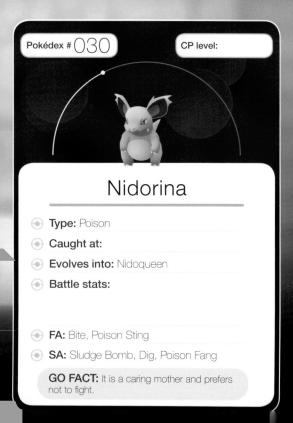

Pokédex # 030 CP level:

Nidorina

- **Type:** Poison
- **Caught at:**
- **Evolves into:** Nidoqueen
- **Battle stats:**

- **FA:** Bite, Poison Sting
- **SA:** Sludge Bomb, Dig, Poison Fang

  GO FACT: It is a caring mother and prefers not to fight.

Pokédex # 031 CP level:

Nidoqueen

- **Type:** Poison / Ground
- **Caught at:**
- **Evolves into:** N/A
- **Battle stats:**

- **FA:** Bite, Poison Jab
- **SA:** Stone Edge, Earthquake, Sludge Wave

  GO FACT: Its body is covered in extremely hard scales.

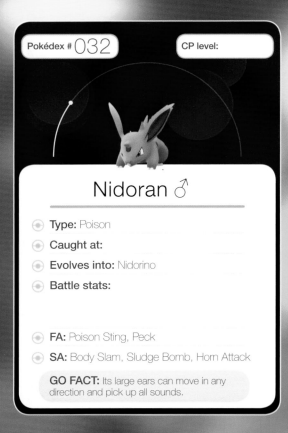

Nidoran ♂

- **Type:** Poison
- **Caught at:**
- **Evolves into:** Nidorino
- **Battle stats:**

- **FA:** Poison Sting, Peck
- **SA:** Body Slam, Sludge Bomb, Horn Attack

GO FACT: Its large ears can move in any direction and pick up all sounds.

Pokédex # 032 — CP level:

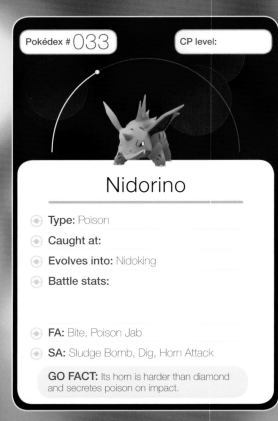

Nidorino

- **Type:** Poison
- **Caught at:**
- **Evolves into:** Nidoking
- **Battle stats:**

- **FA:** Bite, Poison Jab
- **SA:** Sludge Bomb, Dig, Horn Attack

GO FACT: Its horn is harder than diamond and secretes poison on impact.

Pokédex # 033 — CP level:

Clefable

- **Type:** Fairy
- **Caught at:**
- **Evolves into:** N/A
- **Battle stats:**

- **FA:** Pound, Zen Headbutt
- **SA:** Moonblast, Psychic, Dazzling Gleam

GO FACT: It has extremely good hearing.

Pokédex # 036 — CP level:

Vulpix

- **Type:** Fire
- **Caught at:**
- **Evolves into:** Ninetales
- **Battle stats:**

- **FA:** Ember, Quick Attack
- **SA:** Body Slam, Flamethrower, Flame Charge

GO FACT: Its tails grow hot as it nears evolution.

Pokédex # 037 — CP level:

Pokédex # 034 — CP level:

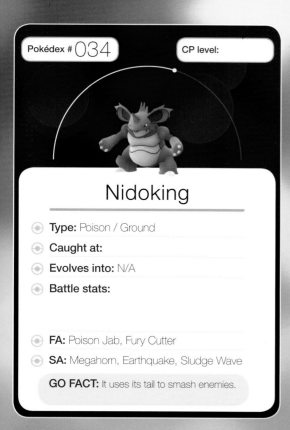

Nidoking

- **Type:** Poison / Ground
- **Caught at:**
- **Evolves into:** N/A
- **Battle stats:**

- **FA:** Poison Jab, Fury Cutter
- **SA:** Megahorn, Earthquake, Sludge Wave

GO FACT: It uses its tail to smash enemies.

Pokédex # 035 — CP level:

Clefairy

- **Type:** Fairy
- **Caught at:**
- **Evolves into:** Clefable
- **Battle stats:**

- **FA:** Pound, Zen Headbutt
- **SA:** Body Slam, Moonblast, Disarming Voice

GO FACT: Clefairy's wings store moonlight and allow it to float.

Pokédex # 038 — CP level:

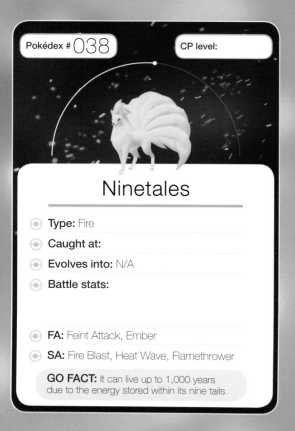

Ninetales

- **Type:** Fire
- **Caught at:**
- **Evolves into:** N/A
- **Battle stats:**

- **FA:** Feint Attack, Ember
- **SA:** Fire Blast, Heat Wave, Flamethrower

GO FACT: It can live up to 1,000 years due to the energy stored within its nine tails.

Pokédex # 039 — CP level:

Jigglypuff

- **Type:** Normal / Fairy
- **Caught at:**
- **Evolves into:** Wigglytuff
- **Battle stats:**

- **FA:** Pound, Feint Attack
- **SA:** Body Slam, Play Rough, Disarming Voice

GO FACT: It sings at its foes to make them drowsy.

Pokédex # 040

CP level:

Wigglytuff

- **Type:** Normal / Fairy
- **Caught at:**
- **Evolves into:** N/A
- **Battle stats:**

- **FA:** Pound, Feint Attack
- **SA:** Hyper Beam, Play Rough, Dazzling Gleam

GO FACT: It can inflate its body by inhaling.

Pokédex # 041

CP level:

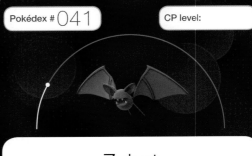

Zubat

- **Type:** Poison / Flying
- **Caught at:**
- **Evolves into:** Golbat
- **Battle stats:**

- **FA:** Bite, Quick Attack
- **SA:** Sludge Bomb, Poison Fang, Air Cutter

GO FACT: It doesn't have any eyes and navigates by echolocation.

Pokédex # 044

CP level:

Gloom

- **Type:** Grass / Poison
- **Caught at:**
- **Evolves into:** Vileplume
- **Battle stats:**

- **FA:** Razor Leaf, Acid
- **SA:** Sludge Bomb, Moonblast, Petal Blizzard

GO FACT: The flower on its head releases a foul odor that can make humans faint.

Pokédex # 045

CP level:

Vileplume

- **Type:** Grass / Poison
- **Caught at:**
- **Evolves into:** N/A
- **Battle stats:**

- **FA:** Razor Leaf, Acid
- **SA:** Solar Beam, Sludge Bomb, Moonblast

GO FACT: Vileplume's flower is said to have the largest petals in the world.

Golbat

Pokédex # 042

CP level:

- **Type:** Poison / Flying
- **Caught at:**
- **Evolves into:** N/A
- **Battle stats:**

- **FA:** Wing Attack, Bite
- **SA:** Poison Fang, Ominous Wind, Air Cutter

GO FACT: It feeds on the blood of Pokémon and humans.

Oddish

Pokédex # 043

CP level:

- **Type:** Grass / Poison
- **Caught at:**
- **Evolves into:** Gloom
- **Battle stats:**

- **FA:** Razor Leaf, Acid
- **SA:** Sludge Bomb, Moonblast, Seed Bomb

GO FACT: Its leaves absorb moonlight, which allows it to grow.

Paras

Pokédex # 046

CP level:

- **Type:** Bug / Grass
- **Caught at:**
- **Evolves into:** Parasect
- **Battle stats:**

- **FA:** Scratch, Bug Bite
- **SA:** Seed Bomb, Cross Poison, X Scissor

GO FACT: The mushrooms on its back can be removed and used as medicine.

Parasect

Pokédex # 047

CP level:

- **Type:** Bug / Grass
- **Caught at:**
- **Evolves into:** N/A
- **Battle stats:**

- **FA:** Bug Bite, Fury Cutter
- **SA:** Solar Beam, Cross Poison, X Scissor

GO FACT: Parasect has been taken over by the mushroom on its back.

Pokédex # 048

CP level:

Venonat

- ⊙ **Type:** Bug / Poison
- ⊙ **Caught at:**
- ⊙ **Evolves into:** Venomoth
- ⊙ **Battle stats:**

- ⊙ **FA:** Bug Bite, Confusion
- ⊙ **SA:** Signal Beam, Psybeam, Poison Fang

GO FACT: It has highly developed eyes that can shoot out laser beams.

Pokédex # 049

CP level:

Venomoth

- ⊙ **Type:** Bug / Poison
- ⊙ **Caught at:**
- ⊙ **Evolves into:** N/A
- ⊙ **Battle stats:**

- ⊙ **FA:** Bug Bite, Confusion
- ⊙ **SA:** Psychic, Bug Buzz, Poison Fang

GO FACT: Its wings are covered in toxic scales.

Pokédex # 052

CP level:

Meowth

- ⊙ **Type:** Normal
- ⊙ **Caught at:**
- ⊙ **Evolves into:** Persian
- ⊙ **Battle stats:**

- ⊙ **FA:** Scratch, Bite
- ⊙ **SA:** Body Slam, Dark Pulse, Night Slash

GO FACT: Meowth is attracted to round, shiny objects.

Pokédex # 053

CP level:

Persian

- ⊙ **Type:** Normal
- ⊙ **Caught at:**
- ⊙ **Evolves into:** N/A
- ⊙ **Battle stats:**

- ⊙ **FA:** Scratch, Feint Attack
- ⊙ **SA:** Play Rough, Power Gem, Night Slash

GO FACT: It can walk without making a sound.

Diglett

Pokédex # 050   CP level:

- **Type:** Ground
- **Caught at:**
- **Evolves into:** Dugtrio
- **Battle stats:**

- **FA:** Scratch, Mud Shot
- **SA:** Dig, Mud Bomb, Rock Tomb

GO FACT: If Diglett is exposed to sunlight, it will heat up and grow weak.

Dugtrio

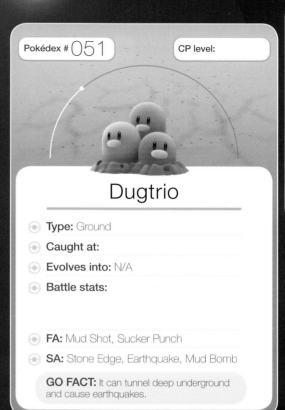

Pokédex # 051   CP level:

- **Type:** Ground
- **Caught at:**
- **Evolves into:** N/A
- **Battle stats:**

- **FA:** Mud Shot, Sucker Punch
- **SA:** Stone Edge, Earthquake, Mud Bomb

GO FACT: It can tunnel deep underground and cause earthquakes.

Psyduck

Pokédex # 054   CP level:

- **Type:** Water
- **Caught at:**
- **Evolves into:** Golduck
- **Battle stats:**

- **FA:** Water Gun, Zen Headbutt
- **SA:** Cross Chop, Aqua Tail, Psybeam

GO FACT: It has an intense headache but can release tension in the form of psychic powers.

Golduck

Pokédex # 055   CP level:

- **Type:** Water
- **Caught at:**
- **Evolves into:** N/A
- **Battle stats:**

- **FA:** Water Gun, Confusion
- **SA:** Hydro Pump, Psychic, Ice Beam

GO FACT: Golduck is an excellent swimmer and can outswim humans.

Pokédex # 056   CP level:

Mankey

- **Type:** Fighting
- **Caught at:**
- **Evolves into:** Primeape
- **Battle stats:**

- **FA:** Scratch, Karate Chop
- **SA:** Cross Chop, Brick Break, Low Sweep

GO FACTS: It is very aggressive and likes eating chestnuts and bananas.

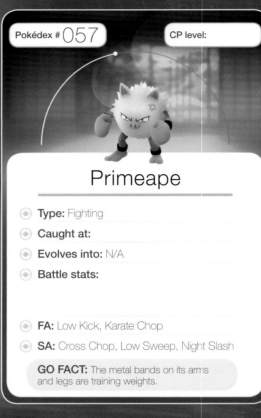

Pokédex # 057   CP level:

Primeape

- **Type:** Fighting
- **Caught at:**
- **Evolves into:** N/A
- **Battle stats:**

- **FA:** Low Kick, Karate Chop
- **SA:** Cross Chop, Low Sweep, Night Slash

GO FACT: The metal bands on its arms and legs are training weights.

Pokédex # 060   CP level:

Poliwag

- **Type:** Water
- **Caught at:**
- **Evolves into:** Poliwhirl
- **Battle stats:**

- **FA:** Mud Shot, Bubble
- **SA:** Body Slam, Mud Bomb, Bubble Beam

GO FACT: The black-and-white swirls on its belly are its internal organs.

Pokédex # 061   CP level:

Poliwhirl

- **Type:** Water
- **Caught at:**
- **Evolves into:** Poliwrath
- **Battle stats:**

- **FA:** Mud Shot, Bubble
- **SA:** Scald, Mud Bomb, Bubble Beam

GO FACT: Its skin is covered in an oily fluid that allows it to slip away from enemies easily.

Pokédex # 058   CP level:

Growlithe

- ◉ **Type:** Fire
- ◉ **Caught at:**
- ◉ **Evolves into:** Arcanine
- ◉ **Battle stats:**

- ◉ **FA:** Bite, Ember
- ◉ **SA:** Body Slam, Flamethrower, Flame Wheel

GO FACT: A friendly and loyal creature, it will always defend its Trainer.

Pokédex # 059   CP level:

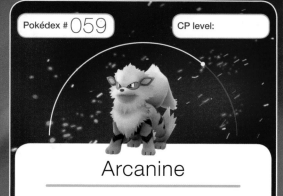

Arcanine

- ◉ **Type:** Fire
- ◉ **Caught at:**
- ◉ **Evolves into:** N/A
- ◉ **Battle stats:**

- ◉ **FA:** Bite, Fire Fang
- ◉ **SA:** Fire Blast, Flamethrower, Bulldoze

GO FACT: It can run 10,000 km in 24 hours.

Pokédex # 062   CP level:

Poliwrath

- ◉ **Type:** Water / Fighting
- ◉ **Caught at:**
- ◉ **Evolves into:** N/A
- ◉ **Battle stats:**

- ◉ **FA:** Mud Shot, Bubble
- ◉ **SA:** Hydro Pump, Submission, Ice Punch

GO FACT: It is able to run briefly on water.

Pokédex # 063   CP level:

Abra

- ◉ **Type:** Psychic
- ◉ **Caught at:**
- ◉ **Evolves into:** Kadabra
- ◉ **Battle stats:**

- ◉ **FA:** Zen Headbutt
- ◉ **SA:** Psyshock, Shadow Ball, Signal Beam

GO FACT: It can sense danger by reading minds.

Pokédex # 064 — CP level:

Kadabra

- **Type:** Psychic
- **Caught at:**
- **Evolves into:** Alakazam
- **Battle stats:**

- **FA:** Psycho Cut, Confusion
- **SA:** Shadow Ball, Dazzling Gleam, Psybeam

GO FACT: It can use its powers to induce headaches.

Pokédex # 065 — CP level:

Alakazam

- **Type:** Psychic
- **Caught at:**
- **Evolves into:** N/A
- **Battle stats:**

- **FA:** Psycho Cut, Confusion
- **SA:** Psychic, Shadow Ball, Dazzling Gleam

GO FACT: The silver spoons it holds amplify its psychic powers.

Pokédex # 068 — CP level:

Machamp

- **Type:** Fighting
- **Caught at:**
- **Evolves into:** N/A
- **Battle stats:**

- **FA:** Bullet Punch, Karate Chop
- **SA:** Cross Chop, Stone Edge, Submission

GO FACT: Four arms allow it to hit attackers at multiple angles.

Pokédex # 069 — CP level:

Bellsprout

- **Type:** Grass / Poison
- **Caught at:**
- **Evolves into:** Weepinbell
- **Battle stats:**

- **FA:** Vine Whip, Acid
- **SA:** Power Whip, Sludge Bomb, Wrap

GO FACT: It can't move when its roots are in the ground.

Pokédex # 066   CP level:

Machop

- **Type:** Fighting
- **Caught at:**
- **Evolves into:** Machoke
- **Battle stats:**

- **FA:** Low Kick, Karate Chop
- **SA:** Cross Chop, Brick Break, Low Sweep

GO FACT: It can lift many times its own body weight.

Pokédex # 067   CP level:

Machoke

- **Type:** Fighting
- **Caught at:**
- **Evolves into:** Machamp
- **Battle stats:**

- **FA:** Low Kick, Karate Chop
- **SA:** Cross Chop, Brick Break, Submission

GO FACT: It wears a power-save belt to regulate its strength.

Pokédex # 070   CP level:

Weepinbell

- **Type:** Grass / Poison
- **Caught at:**
- **Evolves into:** Victreebel
- **Battle stats:**

- **FA:** Razor Leaf, Acid
- **SA:** Power Whip, Sludge Bomb, Seed Bomb

GO FACT: Its razor-sharp leaves can slice up prey.

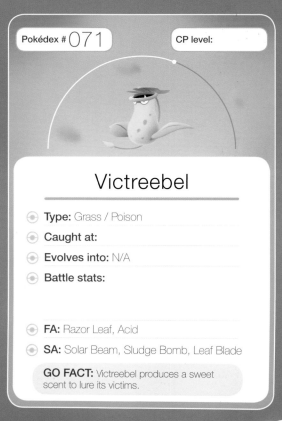

Pokédex # 071   CP level:

Victreebel

- **Type:** Grass / Poison
- **Caught at:**
- **Evolves into:** N/A
- **Battle stats:**

- **FA:** Razor Leaf, Acid
- **SA:** Solar Beam, Sludge Bomb, Leaf Blade

GO FACT: Victreebel produces a sweet scent to lure its victims.

Pokédex # 072

CP level:

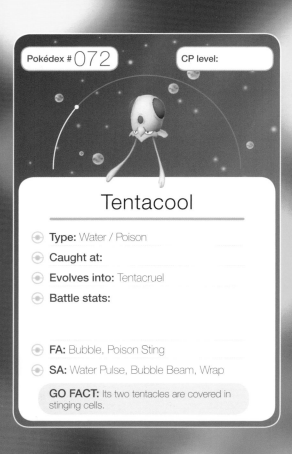

Tentacool

- **Type:** Water / Poison
- **Caught at:**
- **Evolves into:** Tentacruel
- **Battle stats:**

- **FA:** Bubble, Poison Sting
- **SA:** Water Pulse, Bubble Beam, Wrap

GO FACT: Its two tentacles are covered in stinging cells.

Pokédex # 073

CP level:

Tentacruel

- **Type:** Water / Poison
- **Caught at:**
- **Evolves into:** N/A
- **Battle stats:**

- **FA:** Poison Jab, Acid
- **SA:** Blizzard, Hydro Pump, Sludge Wave

GO FACT: Up to eighty toxic tentacles extend from its body.

Pokédex # 076

CP level:

Golem

- **Type:** Rock / Ground
- **Caught at:**
- **Evolves into:** N/A
- **Battle stats:**

- **FA:** Mud Shot, Rock Throw
- **SA:** Stone Edge, Earthquake, Ancient Power

GO FACT: Golem grows bigger by shedding its skin once a year.

Pokédex # 077

CP level:

Ponyta

- **Type:** Fire
- **Caught at:**
- **Evolves into:** Rapidash
- **Battle stats:**

- **FA:** Tackle, Ember
- **SA:** Fire Blast, Flame Wheel, Flame Charge

GO FACT: It can leap over tall buildings with a single jump.

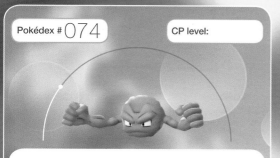

Geodude

Pokédex # 074   CP level:

- **Type:** Rock / Ground
- **Caught at:**
- **Evolves into:** Graveler
- **Battle stats:**

- **FA:** Tackle, Rock Throw
- **SA:** Rock Slide, Dig, Rock Tomb

GO FACT: The longer it lives, the more chipped its body becomes.

Graveler

Pokédex # 075   CP level:

- **Type:** Rock / Ground
- **Caught at:**
- **Evolves into:** Golem
- **Battle stats:**

- **FA:** Mud Shot, Rock Throw
- **SA:** Stone Edge, Rock Slide, Dig

GO FACTS: It grows by eating rocks and rolls down mountains at high speeds.

Rapidash

Pokédex # 078   CP level:

- **Type:** Fire
- **Caught at:**
- **Evolves into:** N/A
- **Battle stats:**

- **FA:** Ember, Low Kick
- **SA:** Fire Blast, Heat Wave, Drill Run

GO FACT: It runs at speeds of about 240 km/h.

Slowpoke

Pokédex # 079   CP level:

- **Type:** Water / Psychic
- **Caught at:**
- **Evolves into:** Slowbro
- **Battle stats:**

- **FA:** Water Gun, Confusion
- **SA:** Psychic, Water Pulse, Psybeam

GO FACT: Slowpoke is not very intelligent and often forgets what it is doing!

Pokédex # 080

CP level:

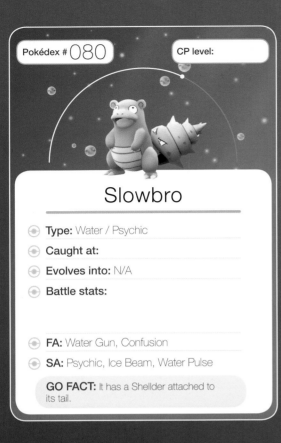

Slowbro

- **Type:** Water / Psychic
- **Caught at:**
- **Evolves into:** N/A
- **Battle stats:**

- **FA:** Water Gun, Confusion
- **SA:** Psychic, Ice Beam, Water Pulse

GO FACT: It has a Shellder attached to its tail.

Pokédex # 081

CP level:

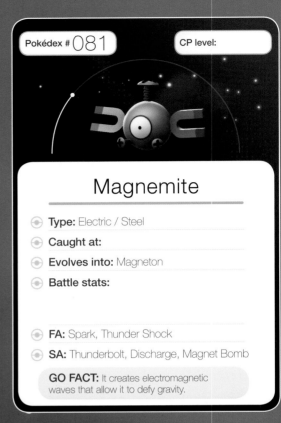

Magnemite

- **Type:** Electric / Steel
- **Caught at:**
- **Evolves into:** Magneton
- **Battle stats:**

- **FA:** Spark, Thunder Shock
- **SA:** Thunderbolt, Discharge, Magnet Bomb

GO FACT: It creates electromagnetic waves that allow it to defy gravity.

Pokédex # 084

CP level:

Doduo

- **Type:** Normal / Flying
- **Caught at:**
- **Evolves into:** Dodrio
- **Battle stats:**

- **FA:** Peck, Quick Attack
- **SA:** Drill Peck, Aerial Ace, Swift

GO FACT: Males have black necks; females have brown necks.

Pokédex # 085

CP level:

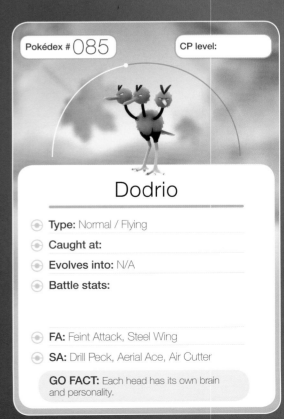

Dodrio

- **Type:** Normal / Flying
- **Caught at:**
- **Evolves into:** N/A
- **Battle stats:**

- **FA:** Feint Attack, Steel Wing
- **SA:** Drill Peck, Aerial Ace, Air Cutter

GO FACT: Each head has its own brain and personality.

Magneton

Pokédex # 082 CP level:

- **Type:** Electric / Steel
- **Caught at:**
- **Evolves into:** N/A
- **Battle stats:**

- **FA:** Spark, Thunder Shock
- **SA:** Flash Cannon, Discharge, Magnet Bomb

GO FACT: Magneton is three Magnemites linked together by magnetic force.

Farfetch'd

Pokédex # 083 CP level:

CATCHABLE ONLY IN ASIA

- **Type:** Normal / Flying
- **Caught at:**
- **Evolves into:** N/A
- **Battle stats:**

- **FA:** Cut, Fury Cutter
- **SA:** Leaf Blade, Aerial Ace, Air Cutter

GO FACT: Farfetch'd will defend the plant stalk it carries with its life.

Seel

Pokédex # 086 CP level:

- **Type:** Water
- **Caught at:**
- **Evolves into:** Dewgong
- **Battle stats:**

- **FA:** Water Gun, Ice Shard
- **SA:** Aqua Tail, Aqua Jet, Icy Wind

GO FACT: It uses the spike on its head to punch through ice.

Dewgong

Pokédex # 087 CP level:

- **Type:** Water / Ice
- **Caught at:**
- **Evolves into:** N/A
- **Battle stats:**

- **FA:** Frost Breath, Ice Shard
- **SA:** Blizzard, Aqua Jet, Icy Wind

GO FACT: It becomes more active the colder the temperature gets.

Pokédex # 088

CP level:

Grimer

- ⊙ **Type:** Poison
- ⊙ **Caught at:**
- ⊙ **Evolves into:** Muk
- ⊙ **Battle stats:**

- ⊙ **FA:** Mud Slap, Acid
- ⊙ **SA:** Sludge Bomb, Sludge, Mud Bomb

GO FACT: Because Grimer doesn't have a solid form, it can squeeze into any space.

Pokédex # 089

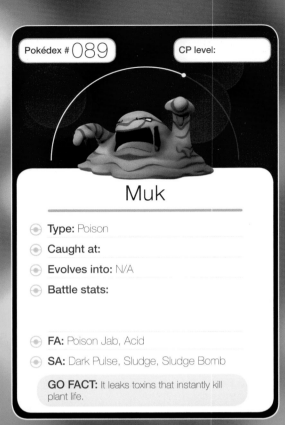

CP level:

Muk

- ⊙ **Type:** Poison
- ⊙ **Caught at:**
- ⊙ **Evolves into:** N/A
- ⊙ **Battle stats:**

- ⊙ **FA:** Poison Jab, Acid
- ⊙ **SA:** Dark Pulse, Sludge, Sludge Bomb

GO FACT: It leaks toxins that instantly kill plant life.

Pokédex # 092

CP level:

Gastly

- ⊙ **Type:** Ghost / Poison
- ⊙ **Caught at:**
- ⊙ **Evolves into:** Haunter
- ⊙ **Battle stats:**

- ⊙ **FA:** Lick, Sucker Punch
- ⊙ **SA:** Sludge Bomb, Dark Pulse, Ominous Wind

GO FACT: Its body is 95% poisonous gas.

Pokédex # 093

CP level:

Haunter

- ⊙ **Type:** Ghost / Poison
- ⊙ **Caught at:**
- ⊙ **Evolves into:** Gengar
- ⊙ **Battle stats:**

- ⊙ **FA:** Shadow Claw, Lick
- ⊙ **SA:** Sludge Bomb, Shadow Ball, Dark Pulse

GO FACT: It can float through solid walls.

Shellder

Pokédex # 090 CP level:

- **Type:** Water
- **Caught at:**
- **Evolves into:** Cloyster
- **Battle stats:**

- **FA:** Tackle, Ice Shard
- **SA:** Water Pulse, Bubble Beam, Icy Wind

GO FACT: Its long tongue can lure and capture prey.

Cloyster

Pokédex # 091 CP level:

- **Type:** Water / Ice
- **Caught at:**
- **Evolves into:** N/A
- **Battle stats:**

- **FA:** Frost Breath, Ice Shard
- **SA:** Blizzard, Hydro Pump, Icy Wind

GO FACT: Its shell is harder than diamond.

Gengar

Pokédex # 094 CP level:

- **Type:** Ghost / Poison
- **Caught at:**
- **Evolves into:** N/A
- **Battle stats:**

- **FA:** Shadow Claw, Sucker Punch
- **SA:** Sludge Wave, Shadow Ball, Dark Pulse

GO FACT: It can hide in the shadow of any object.

Onix

Pokédex # 095 CP level:

- **Type:** Rock / Ground
- **Caught at:**
- **Evolves into:** N/A
- **Battle stats:**

- **FA:** Tackle, Rock Throw
- **SA:** Stone Edge, Rock Slide, Iron Head

GO FACT: Onix tunnels underground and eats boulders as it goes.

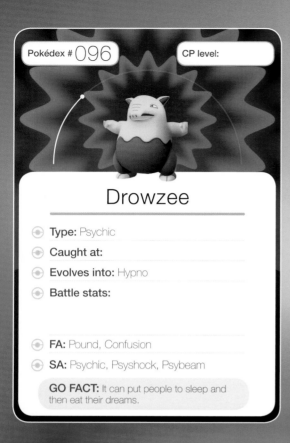

Drowzee

Pokédex # 096

CP level:

- **Type:** Psychic
- **Caught at:**
- **Evolves into:** Hypno
- **Battle stats:**

- **FA:** Pound, Confusion
- **SA:** Psychic, Psyshock, Psybeam

GO FACT: It can put people to sleep and then eat their dreams.

Hypno

Pokédex # 097

CP level:

- **Type:** Psychic
- **Caught at:**
- **Evolves into:** N/A
- **Battle stats:**

- **FA:** Zen Headbutt, Confusion
- **SA:** Psychic, Psyshock, Shadow Ball

GO FACT: Its pendulum is used to hypnotize prey.

Voltorb

Pokédex # 100

CP level:

- **Type:** Electric
- **Caught at:**
- **Evolves into:** Electrode
- **Battle stats:**

- **FA:** Tackle, Spark
- **SA:** Thunderbolt, Signal Beam, Discharge

GO FACT: It is thought that Voltorb was created from a Poké Ball.

Electrode

Pokédex # 101

CP level:

- **Type:** Electric
- **Caught at:**
- **Evolves into:** N/A
- **Battle stats:**

- **FA:** Tackle, Spark
- **SA:** Hyper Beam, Thunderbolt, Discharge

GO FACT: The more electricity it consumes, the faster it moves.

Card 1

Pokédex # 098

CP level:

Krabby

- **Type:** Water
- **Caught at:**
- **Evolves into:** Kingler
- **Battle stats:**

- **FA:** Mud Shot, Bubble
- **SA:** Vice Grip, Water Pulse, Bubble Beam

GO FACT: If Krabby loses a claw, it can regrow it over a short period.

Card 2

Pokédex # 099

CP level:

Kingler

- **Type:** Water
- **Caught at:**
- **Evolves into:** N/A
- **Battle stats:**

- **FA:** Metal Claw, Mud Shot
- **SA:** X Scissor, Vice Grip, Water Pulse

GO FACT: Its left claw is twice the size of the right and as strong as steel.

Card 3

Pokédex # 102

CP level:

Exeggcute

- **Type:** Grass / Psychic
- **Caught at:**
- **Evolves into:** Exeggutor
- **Battle stats:**

- **FA:** Confusion
- **SA:** Psychic, Seed Bomb, Ancient Power

GO FACT: The six heads communicate by telepathy.

Card 4

Pokédex # 103

CP level:

Exeggutor

- **Type:** Grass / Psychic
- **Caught at:**
- **Evolves into:** N/A
- **Battle stats:**

- **FA:** Zen Headbutt, Confusion
- **SA:** Solar Beam, Psychic, Seed Bomb

GO FACT: A head that grows too large and falls off will become an Exeggcute again.

Pokédex # 104   CP level:

Cubone

- **Type:** Ground
- **Caught at:**
- **Evolves into:** Marowak
- **Battle stats:**

- **FA:** Mud Slap, Rock Smash
- **SA:** Bone Club, Dig, Bulldoze

GO FACT: It wears the skull of its dead mother as a helmet.

Pokédex # 105   CP level:

Marowak

- **Type:** Ground
- **Caught at:**
- **Evolves into:** N/A
- **Battle stats:**

- **FA:** Mud Slap, Rock Smash
- **SA:** Earthquake, Bone Club, Dig

GO FACT: It uses its bone as a weapon and a boomerang.

Pokédex # 108   CP level:

Lickitung

- **Type:** Normal
- **Caught at:**
- **Evolves into:** N/A
- **Battle stats:**

- **FA:** Zen Headbutt, Lick
- **SA:** Power Whip, Hyper Beam, Stomp

GO FACT: Its tongue is twice as long as its body.

Pokédex # 109   CP level:

Koffing

- **Type:** Poison
- **Caught at:**
- **Evolves into:** Weezing
- **Battle stats:**

- **FA:** Tackle, Acid
- **SA:** Sludge Bomb, Dark Pulse, Sludge

GO FACT: Koffing is filled with toxic gases that allow it to hover.

Pokédex # 106 — CP level:

Hitmonlee

- **Type:** Fighting
- **Caught at:**
- **Evolves into:** N/A
- **Battle stats:**

- **FA:** Rock Smash, Low Kick
- **SA:** Stone Edge, Stomp, Low Sweep

GO FACT: Its legs stretch like a coiled spring to kick opponents.

Pokédex # 107 — CP level:

Hitmonchan

- **Type:** Fighting
- **Caught at:**
- **Evolves into:** N/A
- **Battle stats:**

- **FA:** Rock Smash, Bullet Punch
- **SA:** Brick Break, Thunder Punch, Fire Punch, Ice Punch

GO FACT: Hitmonchan has the spirit of a boxer and specializes in punching.

Pokédex # 110 — CP level:

Weezing

- **Type:** Poison
- **Caught at:**
- **Evolves into:** N/A
- **Battle stats:**

- **FA:** Tackle, Acid
- **SA:** Sludge Bomb, Shadow Ball, Dark Pulse

GO FACT: Weezing forms when poison gases mix and two Koffings fuse together.

Pokédex # 111 — CP level:

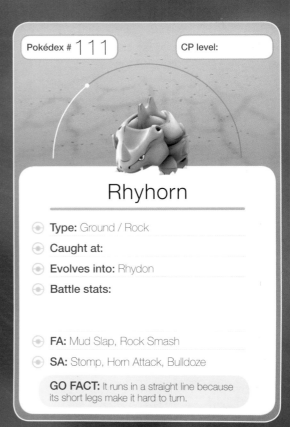

Rhyhorn

- **Type:** Ground / Rock
- **Caught at:**
- **Evolves into:** Rhydon
- **Battle stats:**

- **FA:** Mud Slap, Rock Smash
- **SA:** Stomp, Horn Attack, Bulldoze

GO FACT: It runs in a straight line because its short legs make it hard to turn.

Rhydon

Pokédex # 112   CP level:

- ⊙ **Type:** Ground / Rock
- ⊙ **Caught at:**
- ⊙ **Evolves into:** N/A
- ⊙ **Battle stats:**

- ⊙ **FA:** Mud Slap, Rock Smash
- ⊙ **SA:** Stone Edge, Megahorn, Earthquake

  GO FACTS: Its tail can topple buildings, and its horn can shatter diamond.

Chansey

Pokédex # 113   CP level:

- ⊙ **Type:** Normal
- ⊙ **Caught at:**
- ⊙ **Evolves into:** N/A
- ⊙ **Battle stats:**

- ⊙ **FA:** Pound, Zen Headbutt
- ⊙ **SA:** Psychic, Dazzling Gleam, Psybeam

  GO FACT: Chansey is a female-only species.

Horsea

Pokédex # 116   CP level:

- ⊙ **Type:** Water
- ⊙ **Caught at:**
- ⊙ **Evolves into:** Seadra
- ⊙ **Battle stats:**

- ⊙ **FA:** Water Gun, Bubble
- ⊙ **SA:** Dragon Pulse, Flash Cannon, Bubble Beam

  GO FACT: It can spray water or black ink from its mouth at attackers.

Seadra

Pokédex # 117   CP level:

- ⊙ **Type:** Water
- ⊙ **Caught at:**
- ⊙ **Evolves into:** N/A
- ⊙ **Battle stats:**

- ⊙ **FA:** Water Gun, Dragon Breath
- ⊙ **SA:** Blizzard, Hydro Pump, Dragon Pulse

  GO FACT: It can spin its body to create large whirlpools to catch prey.

Pokédex # 114

CP level:

Tangela

- **Type:** Grass
- **Caught at:**
- **Evolves into:** N/A
- **Battle stats:**

- **FA:** Vine Whip
- **SA:** Power Whip, Solar Beam, Sludge Bomb

GO FACT: Thick blue vines cover its body, so no one knows what it looks like underneath.

Pokédex # 115

CP level:

CATCHABLE ONLY IN AUSTRALIA AND NEW ZEALAND

Kangaskhan

- **Type:** Normal
- **Caught at:**
- **Evolves into:** N/A
- **Battle stats:**

- **FA:** Mud Slap, Low Kick
- **SA:** Earthquake, Brick Break, Stomp

GO FACT: It sleeps standing up so as not to crush the baby in its pouch.

Pokédex # 118

CP level:

Goldeen

- **Type:** Water
- **Caught at:**
- **Evolves into:** Seaking
- **Battle stats:**

- **FA:** Mud Shot, Peck
- **SA:** Aqua Tail, Horn Attack, Water Pulse

GO FACT: It uses its horn to smash its way to freedom.

Pokédex # 119

CP level:

Seaking

- **Type:** Water
- **Caught at:**
- **Evolves into:** N/A
- **Battle stats:**

- **FA:** Water Gun, Quick Attack
- **SA:** Megahorn, Drill Run, Icy Wind

GO FACT: It can swim up waterfalls.

Staryu

Pokédex # 120	**CP level:**

- **Type:** Water
- **Caught at:**
- **Evolves into:** Starmie
- **Battle stats:**

- **FA:** Water Gun, Quick Attack
- **SA:** Power Gem, Bubble Beam, Swift

GO FACT: Its core shines brightest at nighttime.

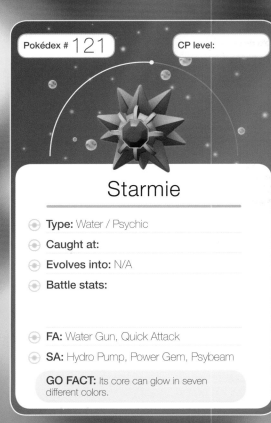

Starmie

Pokédex # 121	**CP level:**

- **Type:** Water / Psychic
- **Caught at:**
- **Evolves into:** N/A
- **Battle stats:**

- **FA:** Water Gun, Quick Attack
- **SA:** Hydro Pump, Power Gem, Psybeam

GO FACT: Its core can glow in seven different colors.

Jynx

Pokédex # 124	**CP level:**

- **Type:** Ice / Psychic
- **Caught at:**
- **Evolves into:** N/A
- **Battle stats:**

- **FA:** Pound, Frost Breath
- **SA:** Psyshock, Psybeam, Draining Kiss

GO FACT: Jynx likes to communicate through dance moves.

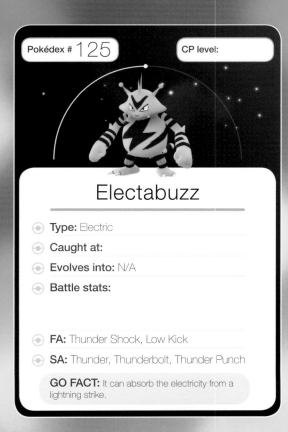

Electabuzz

Pokédex # 125	**CP level:**

- **Type:** Electric
- **Caught at:**
- **Evolves into:** N/A
- **Battle stats:**

- **FA:** Thunder Shock, Low Kick
- **SA:** Thunder, Thunderbolt, Thunder Punch

GO FACT: It can absorb the electricity from a lightning strike.

Pokédex # 122   CP level:

CATCHABLE ONLY IN EUROPE

Mr. Mime

- **Type:** Psychic / Fairy
- **Caught at:**
- **Evolves into:** N/A
- **Battle stats:**

- **FA:** Confusion, Zen Headbutt
- **SA:** Psychic, Shadow Ball, Psybeam

GO FACT: Mr. Mime is a master of pantomime and can create objects out of thin air.

Pokédex # 123   CP level:

Scyther

- **Type:** Bug / Flying
- **Caught at:**
- **Evolves into:** N/A
- **Battle stats:**

- **FA:** Steel Wing, Fury Cutter
- **SA:** Bug Buzz, X Scissor, Night Slash

GO FACT: It uses the scythes on its arms for hunting and fighting.

Pokédex # 126   CP level:

Magmar

- **Type:** Fire
- **Caught at:**
- **Evolves into:** N/A
- **Battle stats:**

- **FA:** Ember, Karate Chop
- **SA:** Fire Blast, Flamethrower, Fire Punch

GO FACT: Its body temperature reaches nearly 1,200°C.

Pokédex # 127   CP level:

Pinsir

- **Type:** Bug
- **Caught at:**
- **Evolves into:** N/A
- **Battle stats:**

- **FA:** Rock Smash, Fury Cutter
- **SA:** X Scissor, Submission, Vice Grip

GO FACT: It uses its pincers to lift objects twice its weight.

Pokédex # 128   CP level:

CATCHABLE ONLY IN NORTH AMERICA

Tauros

- **Type:** Normal
- **Caught at:**
- **Evolves into:** N/A
- **Battle stats:**

- **FA:** Zen Headbutt, Tackle
- **SA:** Earthquake, Iron Head, Horn Attack

GO FACT: Once it starts charging, Tauros cannot stop until it hits something.

Pokédex # 129   CP level:

Magikarp

- **Type:** Water
- **Caught at:**
- **Evolves into:** Gyarados
- **Battle stats:**

- **FA:** Splash
- **SA:** Struggle

GO FACT: Magikarp is weak and an easy target for predators like Pidgeot.

Pokédex # 132   CP level:

?

Ditto

NOT YET CATCHABLE

- **Type:** Normal
- **Caught at:**
- **Evolves into:** N/A
- **Battle stats:**

- **FA:** Pound
- **SA:** Struggle

GO FACT: It can transform into a replica of any object.

Pokédex # 133   CP level:

Eevee

- **Type:** Normal
- **Caught at:**
- **Evolves into:** Vaporeon, Jolteon, or Flareon
- **Battle stats:**

- **FA:** Tackle, Quick Attack
- **SA:** Body Slam, Dig, Swift

GO FACT: Eevee is mostly found in cities and towns.

Pokédex # 130 — CP level:

Gyarados

- **Type:** Water / Flying
- **Caught at:**
- **Evolves into:** N/A
- **Battle stats:**

- **FA:** Bite, Dragon Breath
- **SA:** Hydro Pump, Dragon Pulse, Twister

GO FACTS: Its fangs can crush stones, and its scales are harder than steel.

Pokédex # 131 — CP level:

Lapras

- **Type:** Water / Ice
- **Caught at:**
- **Evolves into:** N/A
- **Battle stats:**

- **FA:** Frost Breath, Ice Shard
- **SA:** Blizzard, Dragon Pulse, Ice Beam

GO FACT: Lapras is a gentle, helpful Pokémon that can carry humans on its back.

Pokédex # 134 — CP level:

Vaporeon

- **Type:** Water
- **Caught at:**
- **Evolves into:** N/A
- **Battle stats:**

- **FA:** Water Gun
- **SA:** Hydro Pump, Aqua Tail, Water Pulse

GO FACT: It can melt into water molecules, camouflaging it as it swims.

Pokédex # 135 — CP level:

Jolteon

- **Type:** Electric
- **Caught at:**
- **Evolves into:** N/A
- **Battle stats:**

- **FA:** Thunder Shock
- **SA:** Thunder, Thunderbolt, Discharge

GO FACT: Jolteon's electrically charged fur can become sharp like needles.

Pokédex # 136

CP level:

Flareon

- ⊙ **Type:** Fire
- ⊙ **Caught at:**
- ⊙ **Evolves into:** N/A
- ⊙ **Battle stats:**

- ⊙ **FA:** Ember
- ⊙ **SA:** Fire Blast, Heat Wave, Flamethrower

GO FACT: It has an internal flame that gives it a high body temperature.

Pokédex # 137

CP level:

Porygon

- ⊙ **Type:** Normal
- ⊙ **Caught at:**
- ⊙ **Evolves into:** N/A
- ⊙ **Battle stats:**

- ⊙ **FA:** Tackle, Quick Attack
- ⊙ **SA:** Signal Beam, Discharge, Psybeam

GO FACT: Porygon is made out of computer programming code.

Pokédex # 140

CP level:

Kabuto

- ⊙ **Type:** Rock / Water
- ⊙ **Caught at:**
- ⊙ **Evolves into:** Kabutops
- ⊙ **Battle stats:**

- ⊙ **FA:** Scratch, Mud Shot
- ⊙ **SA:** Aqua Jet, Ancient Power, Rock Tomb

GO FACT: It has a powerful swimming ability.

Pokédex # 141

CP level:

Kabutops

- ⊙ **Type:** Rock / Water
- ⊙ **Caught at:**
- ⊙ **Evolves into:** N/A
- ⊙ **Battle stats:**

- ⊙ **FA:** Mud Shot, Fury Cutter
- ⊙ **SA:** Stone Edge, Water Pulse, Ancient Power

GO FACT: It can tuck into its shell to help it swim fast.

Omanyte

Pokédex # 138

CP level:

- **Type:** Rock / Water
- **Caught at:**
- **Evolves into:** Omastar
- **Battle stats:**

- **FA:** Water Gun, Mud Shot
- **SA:** Brine, Ancient Power, Rock Tomb

GO FACT: Gases within its shell regulate its buoyancy in water.

Omastar

Pokédex # 139

CP level:

- **Type:** Rock / Water
- **Caught at:**
- **Evolves into:** N/A
- **Battle stats:**

- **FA:** Water Gun, Rock Throw
- **SA:** Hydro Pump, Rock Slide, Ancient Power

GO FACT: It has a powerful, deadly bite.

Aerodactyl

Pokédex # 142

CP level:

- **Type:** Rock / Flying
- **Caught at:**
- **Evolves into:** N/A
- **Battle stats:**

- **FA:** Bite, Steel Wing
- **SA:** Hyper Beam, Iron Head, Ancient Power

GO FACT: It is extinct in the wild.

Snorlax

Pokédex # 143

CP level:

- **Type:** Normal
- **Caught at:**
- **Evolves into:** N/A
- **Battle stats:**

- **FA:** Zen Headbutt, Lick
- **SA:** Body Slam, Hyper Beam, Earthquake

GO FACT: It only wakes up to eat.

Pokédex # 144 — CP level:

Articuno

- **Type:** Ice / Flying
- **Caught at:**
- **Evolves into:** N/A
- **Battle stats:**

- **FA:** Frost Breath
- **SA:** Blizzard, Ice Beam, Icy Wind

GO FACTS: Articuno is a Legendary bird of Kanto, and its wings are made of ice.

Pokédex # 145 — CP level:

Zapdos

- **Type:** Electric / Flying
- **Caught at:**
- **Evolves into:** N/A
- **Battle stats:**

- **FA:** Thunder Shock
- **SA:** Thunder, Thunderbolt, Discharge

GO FACTS: Zapdos is a Legendary bird of Kanto, and its electricity can cause thunderstorms.

Pokédex # 148 — CP level:

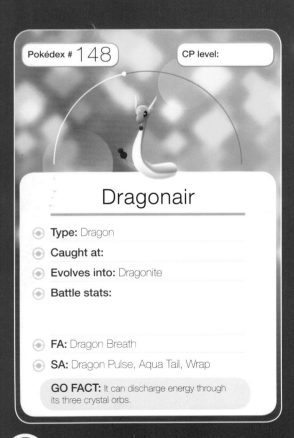

Dragonair

- **Type:** Dragon
- **Caught at:**
- **Evolves into:** Dragonite
- **Battle stats:**

- **FA:** Dragon Breath
- **SA:** Dragon Pulse, Aqua Tail, Wrap

GO FACT: It can discharge energy through its three crystal orbs.

Pokédex # 149 — CP level:

Dragonite

- **Type:** Dragon / Flying
- **Caught at:**
- **Evolves into:** N/A
- **Battle stats:**

- **FA:** Dragon Breath, Steel Wing
- **SA:** Hyper Beam, Dragon Claw, Dragon Pulse

GO FACT: Dragonite can fly faster than the speed of sound.

Moltres

Pokédex # 146   CP level:

NOT YET CATCHABLE

- **Type:** Fire / Flying
- **Caught at:**
- **Evolves into:** N/A
- **Battle stats:**

- **FA:** Ember
- **SA:** Fire Blast, Heat Wave, Flamethrower

GO FACTS: Moltres is a Legendary bird of Kanto, and its wings are covered in fire.

Dratini

Pokédex # 147   CP level:

- **Type:** Dragon
- **Caught at:**
- **Evolves into:** Dragonair
- **Battle stats:**

- **FA:** Dragon Breath
- **SA:** Aqua Tail, Twister, Wrap

GO FACT: Dratini is constantly growing and shedding its skin.

Mewtwo

Pokédex # 150   CP level:

NOT YET CATCHABLE

- **Type:** Psychic
- **Caught at:**
- **Evolves into:** N/A
- **Battle stats:**

- **FA:** Psycho Cut, Confusion
- **SA:** Hyper Beam, Psychic, Shadow Ball

GO FACT: It was created by science to be the ultimate Pokémon in battle.

Mew

Pokédex # 151   CP level:

NOT YET CATCHABLE

- **Type:** Psychic
- **Caught at:**
- **Evolves into:** N/A
- **Battle stats:**

- **FA:** Pound
- **SA:** Hurricane, Solar Beam, Fire Blast, Hyper Beam, Earthquake, Thunder, Moonblast, Psychic, Dragon Pulse

GO FACT: It is said to have the DNA of every Pokémon in its body.

TOP TRAINER AWARD

Congratulations! You have successfully completed my training program and are now equipped with the skills to become a Pokémon Master. Go forth and continue to catch, battle, and train these magical creatures.

This certificate is the official documentation of the hours you have put in as a Trainer, so keep it safe. Fill in the details so I can also keep a record of your achievements.

Pokémon Trainer Certification

Date:

Trainer name: *Tristan07078*

Level reached:

Team: *Mystic*

First Pokémon caught: *squrtle*

Latest Pokémon caught:

Total number of Pokémon caught:

Area-specific Pokémon caught:

Total medals won:

Gold –

Silver –

Bronze –

Gym membership total:

Quiz result: *20*/20

I confirm that the Pokémon training program has been successfully completed and that this Trainer has a bright future ahead of them.

Signed:

Professor Willow

Quiz answers: 1b, 2c, 3a, 4a, 5c, 6a, 7b, 8c, 9b, 10a, 11a, 12c, 13b, 14c, 15b, 16a, 17c, 18b, 19a, 20a